WILLIAM PEAKE

THE EMPIRE OF AUSTRIA DURING ITS LATE REVOLUTIONARY CRISIS

VOLUME II

Elibron Classics
www.elibron.com

Elibron Classics series.

ISBN 0-543-95961-9 (paperback)
ISBN 0-543-95960-0 (hardcover)

This Elibron Classics Replica Edition is an unabridged facsimile of the edition published in 1851 by T. C. Newby, London.

THE
EMPIRE OF AUSTRIA

DURING ITS

LATE REVOLUTIONARY CRISIS.

BY

WILLIAM PEAKE, ESQ.

IN TWO VOLUMES.—VOL. II.

LONDON:
T. C. NEWBY, PUBLISHER,
30, WELBECK STREET.
1851.

THE AUSTRIAN EMPIRE

[DURING ITS LATE

REVOLUTIONARY CRISIS.

CHAPTER I.

AUSTRIA, formerly no naval power, had, by the acquisition of Venice, obtained the maritime arsenal of this bygone republic, and with the same, the means for the formation of a small navy. Those means were, in the course of time, so much furthered that this navy sufficed for the protection of her own merchantmen, and the maintenance of her own seas against the violations of those states with whom, on the agitation of any question of importance, she could, in the main point, obtain her aim on terrâ firmâ. After the revolution at Venice, in the spring of the year 1848, the Austrian fleet still consisted of three frigates, two corvettes, five brigs, one steamer, two galliots, eight gun-boats, and nineteen coasters; altogether, forty vessels. Into the hands of the Venetians had fallen three corvettes, three brigs, twelve gun-boats, two steamers, and a great number of small craft, used for the defence of the Lagunes, as well as a frigate still on the stocks.

On the eastern coast of the Adriatic, opposite to Venice, in a south-easterly direction, lies Pola. Here, now, by the direction of General Nugent, the remaining part of the fleet belonging to Austria was concentrated: its crews were re-organized, and the harbour itself secured by new works. In the first days of May, a Sardinian squadron of three frigates, one brig, one galliot, and two steamers, had appeared in the Gulf of Venice, followed by six men-of-war. Eight days later, they were joined by two frigates, one brig, and five large steamers arriving from Naples. Thus, the Austrian vessels were hindered from co-operating with the land forces against Venice, and even limited to the necessary measures for their own preservation.

The progress of the Austrian arms on the Venetian continent had, for some time, been looked for with anxiety by the home government. Palmanuova, Osopo, and Treviso, remained in the possession of the revolutionists; but at the end of this month a new reserve corps, under General Weldon, received orders to accomplish the conquest of the upper part of the Venetian territory. This corps consisted of sixteen battalions, four squadrons, and eight batteries, and had been concentrated, for the most part, on the Piave. The town of Treviso was observed by a chain of outposts, but its connection with Venice could not be entirely interrupted; and one such post of observation at Portegrandi, at the mouth of the Sile, was surprised in a sally, and the Croats driven from thence. The garrison of Treviso was able to obtain cattle and provisions in the surrounding villages, and they even at times seized the requisitions of the Austrians themselves.

General Weldon had proceeded to Trieste and Görz, in order to make the necessary arrangements for securing provisions and other requisitions for his army, and to ascertain, in person, the exact state of things before Palmanuova, and, in general, in the rear of his line of operations. For the bombardment of Palmanuova, ordered by him, the Austrians had but one mortar at their disposal; but the dexterity of its service, and the perseverance of the blockading corps, caused, in a great measure, the surrender of this important place, notwithstanding that it was defended by three thousand men.

The consequences of this surrender to the Austrians were enormous; for one hundred and fifty-six pieces of heavy artillery fell into their possession The Austrians allowed General Zuchi his liberty, contrary to whose will the citizens—terrified by the approaching want of provisions, the actual blockade, the threatened bombardment, and backed by the discontent of the garrison—had brought about the capitulation; and those soldiers who had belonged to Austrian regiments were sent to their homes. The volunteers obtained a free marching off to Venice, and the Piedmontese were embarked for Genoa, taking a pledge not to serve against Austria for the space of one year. A further order of the commander bore reference to the recovery of the mountainous regions.

In the first days of June a column, consisting of a battalion, four companies, and some rocket pieces, marched on the Tagliamento up-stream to Ampezzo, in order to attack the valley of Codorine from this side. The insurgents had occupied Monte Maura, but were dispersed after a short fight; the principal place, Pieve di Cadore, was taken, and in this manner the communication on the high road from Belluno to Carinthia made free.

In the meanwhile, General Weldon had arrived at Conegliano, and reinforced the division of troops stationed at Belluno, and which, in connection with the troops from Ampezzo, accomplished the subjection of the insurgents in this district. He now advanced for the investment of Treviso. On his left he ordered Portegrandi to be re-occupied, but his right wing proceeded from Crespano and Asolo towards Bassano; a division of fifteen hundred men encamped at Fossa, at this side of the town, and a detachment was advanced as far as

Marostica, which place they occupied. The road from Bassano to Val Sugana and the Tyrol leads directly from the upper part of the town along the Brenta, through a narrow valley called the Canal di Brenta; and the entrance to it was blocked up and the road cut through. The Croats made an attempt to go round this defile, over the mountain, but met with such determined resistance that they were obliged to retreat; but on the following day the Austrians advanced from Feltre with eight companies upon Primolano, and occupied this town in the evening. The insurgents were posted opposite, in a strong position, on the right shore of the Brenta, on the mountain.

On the evening of the 8th of June, two companies from Tezze, joined by two other companies from the Tyrolese corps, and a division of sharpshooters and students from Innsbruck, went over the Brenta, ascended the opposite mountain during the night, and got in the rear of the insurgents, who, nevertheless, offered a brave resistance of three hours; but another column, crossing in their front at Pioveza, they were obliged to give in, and abandon four cannons to their assailants. The consequence of this combat was, the possession by the Austrians of the Canal di Brenta, and the renewed communication between Bassano and the Trent. The Austrians had, on the 12th, arrived with a strong brigade at Schio, disarmed the town, forced the passage of the Val d'Orsa, and joined at Roveredo the troops destined for the defence of the Tyrol, which were now designated as the third corps of the army. This reinforcement was not superfluous, for General Zobel had, in his position at Brentino, to sustain a violent attack from the Piedmontese, and found himself obliged to retreat as far as Avio and Madonna della Neve, upon the territory of Tyrol.

In the Venetian plain the subjection of the country by the Austrians progressed; the marching off of the Neapolitans induced the town of Padua to surrender without striking a blow. General Weldon appeared before Treviso on the 15th of June; and as his summons to surrender remained without notice, the town was bombarded, and in the same evening the inhabitants hoisted the white flag, and a capitulation took place, by which the garrison, four thousand one hundred and eighty-five men strong, received a free marching off to the Po. A few days after, General Weldon advanced towards Venice, occupied Mestre, Bodenigo, Mal Contenta, and Cavanella, on the Etch. The communication of the town of the Lagunes with the Venetian continent was now, therefore, debarred, on the extensive circumference from the mouth of the Piave to that of the Etch.

The garrison of the city of Venice and

its numerous forts consisted partly of the troops deserted from the Austrian colours in the spring, partly of such of other Italian states, of numerous volunteers and of its own civica, and it numbered twenty thousand men; the command-in-chief was held by General William Pepe, and the command of the fortress by General Antonini. The Italians, under General Ferrari, attacked the Austrian position at Cavanella on the 7th of July, but were beaten back. A sally was made from Malghera, whereat a Swiss free corps was present; but checked on the front by the first battalion of volunteers from Vienna, and on the flank attacked by three Austrian companies, they were obliged to retreat with great loss under the cannon of the fort. The situation of Venice is such that, not only the attempt to obtain possession of it by a formal siege is next to an impossibility, but even a blockade intended to hinder supplies from entering is of the utmost difficulty—for, in the stormy season of the year, no squadron stationed in the vicinity can hold the sea; so that the Venetians were able to bid defiance to the Austrians, and nothing more could be effected by these latter than to obtain possession of the surrounding country, and which they had now accomplished, for the most part, without any great difficulty or loss.

The Austrians now urged on the fortification of Verona with the greatest energy, but nothing beyond several skirmishes happened to either of the principal armies during several weeks. Each general most anxiously expected reinforcements—those to the Austrians arrived in good time, and their army had now the following divisions:—The first corps was commanded by General Count Wratislaw; the second by General D'Aspre; the third by General Count Thurm, and the fourth by General Culoz; the first reserve corps by General Wocher, and the second by General Weldon. The total force amounted to one hundred and thirty-two thousand men, in one hundred and twenty-six battalions, and sixty squadrons. The cavalry might be rated at from eight to nine thousand horse, and the number of field artillery was two hundred and forty.

The army of Charles Albert preserved its division into two equal corps, under Generals Bava and De Sonnaz. Next to it was the classification in divisions; the first was commanded by Lieutenant-General d'Arvillars; the second by Lieutenant General di Ferrere; the third by Lieutenant-General Count Broglie; and the fourth by the Duke of Genoa. The reserve division was commanded by the Duke of Savoy, and the Lombard division by General Perrone. In this classification is not included the division of General Durando, on the west side of the lake of Garda, nor that of General Pepe in Venice.

There were persons who were astonished at the news of a movement by the king to the Lower Etch, the aim of which was designed to be the total investment of Mantua. Such a dispersion of the army in sight of a concentrated enemy appeared to many inexplicable; but as in many wars strategy is swayed by politics, and led astray, so also here the judgment of the soldier was, perhaps, obliged to yield to the urgencies of the clubbists, towards whom certain obligations had to be fulfilled.

The Austrian brigade had joined again from the Tyrol at Vicenza. In this town General D'Aspre left a garrison of two thousand men, and broke up with his troops for Verona; and now the first and second corps of the army, and the first reserve corps, found themselves concentrated at Verona. The Austrian camp, under the cannons of Verona, extended southward to Santa Catarina, for which reason a bridge was built at Casa Barvi, for the better communication with the left shore.

Charles Albert now made the greatest preparations, which obviously aimed at the total blockade of Mantua; he transferred his head quarters to Roverbello—the division Ferrere marched from the camp of Goito over Curtatone, as far as Gli Angeli, and took up a position before Fort Belfiore, and towards Cerese; from Cerese to the Estate la Parma the Lombard division was placed, and their duty was to observe Fort Pietole. The investment upon the right shore of the Mincio remained imperfect, however, so long as it did not extend to the edge of the river Virgiliana ; and, as General Perrone was careful not to intrust his yet inexperienced troops alone at this isolated and exposed post, a brigade of veterans and a battalion of volunteers were adjoined to them. Upon the whole Piedmontese line a general evolution to the right took place, and the corps at Rivoli got considerably weakened when the Duke of Genoa, with a part of his division, moved towards Monzambano.

The city of Ferrara had lately received a Piedmontese garrison, and a stop had been put to the previously mentioned manner of providing provisions for the citadel, which was still occupied by Austrian troops. The Marshal found himself, therefore, obliged to dispatch thither Prince Liechtenstein, with a brigade strengthened to five thousand men, in order to free the citadel, and restore the agreement which had been entered into for their supply from the town. The Prince steamed over the Po and suddenly appeared before Ferrara, the garrison of which, for the most part, marched off at his appearance. The agreement was, in consequence, soon renewed, and the town pledged itself to provide the citadel with provisions for two months; and, on the day following, the Prince returned with his troops over the Po. It lay in the plan to proceed with them to Governolo, and to fall from thence upon the right flank and rear of the blockading corps before Mantua, and which movement would have been aided by a sally upon the front of the Piedmontese; but, before the Prince could reach Governolo, that post was already in possession of his adversaries, who had beaten the Austrians out of the town, and thereby secured the right flank of the blockading corps. The king had transferred his head-quarters to Marmirolo. The Duke of Savoy advanced with his division to Castel Belforte, and pushed his outposts forward upon Castellaro—the Duke of Genoa marched up at Mozzecano—thus Mantua was invested on the left shore of the Mincio.

As soon as Radetzky felt assured that a great part of the Piedmontese army had extended and scattered itself for the purpose of investing Mantua in the manner here indicated, he determined upon taking the offensive, and fixed the 23rd of July as the day of its beginning; but first of all, he designed that the attention of the Piedmontese should be drawn to the side of Rivoli.

In the newspapers appeared an Austrian bulletin, which, though it inspired courage, yet seemed to indicate a further prolongation of the defensive.

On the evening of the 21st were concentrated twenty-three companies, a rocket battery, and a battery of howitzers (which latter was transported on the backs of mules), on the Monte Baldo, at Arquanegra. On the 22nd the column broke up, and stood in sight of their enemy, who held the heights southward from Ferrara. General Thurm, who commanded these companies, ordered ten of them to ascend the steep height of Val Tredda, which was not accomplished, however, without great loss; but at length they compelled the Piedmontese to retreat to Rivoli.

The Austrians thought they could now proceed by Incanale towards the table land; but at the village of Zuanne, where the road reaches this height, stood three thousand Piedmontese, with four cannon, in an advantageous fortified position. The Austrian troops ascending from the valley of the Etch were received by a lively artillery fire, and their right flank was threatened by hostile columns from Affi over the heights of Ceradello, which caused them to retire; and, indeed, all they could do was to retain their present position, for the Piedmontese had a well-placed artillery, which could not be approached. They managed, however, to repel the successive assaults of their enemy in an *échelon* position. Although this attack of the Austrians remained without signal success, yet the Piedmontese thought it prudent to retire towards Peschiera; for it was now known that at this time the whole forces of Radetzky were moving from the camp and gates of Verona, for a great decisive blow.

The second corps of the Austrian army, forming the right wing, consisted of four infantry brigades and a brigade of cavalry. The three former took their way over Lugagnan and Mancalaqua, towards Sona; the two latter proceeded on the right towards Santa Giustina. The first corps of the army had a similar arrangement.

General Wohlgemuth led his own brigade, together with four infantry brigades, and those of Generals Supplikatz and Strassoldo, with the brigade Clam, General Prince Schwarzenberg was marching, covering the left wing towards Custozza, and, still further to the left, Colonel Wysz was approaching the fortified town of Villa Franca. The first reserve corps advanced as support in the midst of the two corps, towards Rezel, and the reserve batteries followed close. To most of the brigades of infantry a battery and one or two squadrons of cavalry were given. A part of the Austrian plan of operations aimed at the endeavour to force the centre of the hostile line of battle, and to get, at the same time, into possession of the ridge of mountains which extend from Custozza to the Mincio, and so to command the whole plain towards Mantua. On the foremost of the hills on this "terrain," half or three quarters of a league from each other, from north to south, the villages Santa Giustina, Sona, and Sommacampagna, are situated, and Custozza is one league south-west from the latter. Behind these villages rises a second ridge of hills, in which Monte Godio is particularly conspicuous; and in a third lies, on a similar hill, the village San Giorgio in Salice. Lieutenant-General de Sonnaz occupied this favourite position, fortified by sconces and redoubts; but, in proportion to the extent of country, his troops were not sufficiently numerous.

The combat began upon the right wing. After the Piedmontese skirmishers had retired, having done good service, Colonel Pergen led the attack with his brigade and six cannon, to storm the heights of Sona. After a contest of three hours and a half, this place was taken, together with Montabello and the height Madonna del Monte. A sham attack on Santa Giustina was, in consequence of this success, converted into a real one, and the heights there were also gained by the Austrians, and the Piedmontese gave way at Castelnuovo. At the foot of the mountain upon which Sommacampagna is built stand the buildings of Madonna del Saluti, Osteria alla Torre, and Conbiol, and they formed the outworks of the Piedmontese position. These were now attacked. The Piedmontese defended the mountain with three thousand men and four cannon; and they did not content themselves with a lively fire from behind their walls, but endeavoured to retard the attack by an appropriate movement in flank of the advancing skirmishers; but the column following close, put an end to the attempt. The line was in part taken, in part the mountain was gone round, and then the whole body of Austrians at this spot stormed from three sides; the Piedmontese were obliged to evacuate their position, and retired to the road leading to the Mincio. A general advance took place, on the part of the Austrians, as far as San Giorgio in Salice; and here were now their head quarters.

Radetzky had thus succeeded in his first aim; for on the heights from Monte Vento to Custozza his battalions were standing.

On the right shore of the Mincio this hilly land extends towards Castiglione delle Stivigre, and southward forms a projecting angle, upon which Volta is situated. The marshal now took the resolution to pass the Mincio, and take up a position *à cheval* on both sides of the river, with his front towards Mantua; and his head quarters were transferred to the Palazzo Alzarea, a little to the north of Oliosi.

On the 24th of July the reserve corps advanced to Salionze, and the Piedmontese skirmishers were kept at a distance, while a bridge was happily thrown across the river by the pioneers. The Austrians immediately crossed, and fought their way on. The foremost company with great intrepidity forced a cavalry division with the bayonet, and stormed against an eight-pound battery; three of which guns they took and turned against the enemy; a feat which decorated two officers of the regiment with the cross of

Maria Theresa. The four brigades which were ordered for this service crossed during the day; the Austrians had now, therefore, a position on both right and left sides of the Mincio.

Charles Albert was staying at Villafranca. The difficulty of his position did not escape him. He had to choose between a retreat over Goito, and an attack upon Radetzky's left. He chose the latter. With twenty-five thousand men, and seconded by General Bava, he moved to the attack: the guards, under the Duke of Savoy, formed his left wing, behind which stood a brigade as reserve. The cavalry covered the right flank in the plain, on the side towards Verona. This was a most successful move on the part of the Piedmontese, for they repulsed their enemy on all sides; and all who were attacked were obliged to retreat to Verona. The loss of the Austrians was terribly severe. This advantage of the Piedmontese procured them the possession of the foremost ridge of hills, eastward from the Tione; from Custozza to Sommacampagna.

On the news of this disaster Radetzky resolved to give a general battle to Charles Albert, in order to drive him again from the heights of Custozza down to the plain of Villafranca. Most of the troops which had crossed the Mincio were now recalled to the left shore, and the army made backward front: a most difficult evolution. The first corps of the army formed the right, the second the left wing; Valeggio, as the point of support of the right wing of the Austrian army, remained occupied by a strong brigade, and they made the necessary preparations to defend this town to the uttermost. From here, over Monte Vento, as far as the brook Tione, stood the first corps, and the third corps observed Peschiera. In this position, therefore, the marshal made his preparations to give battle on the morrow; but Charles

Albert also thought of continuing his attack, and made his dispositions accordingly.

With the morning of the 25th the sun was scorching hot, it being at eighty-six degrees of Fahrenheit. At eight o'clock General Bava approached the town of Valeggio, but he did not make any attack until the arrival of reinforcements, when a bombardment was ordered, and two assaults attempted; but these were beaten off by the fire from the garrison, and a bold movement of horse in the flank of the assailants. At the moment that the Duke of Genoa was preparing for an attack, he found that he himself had to expect one from Sona and San Giorgio; and towards noon his position near Sommacampagna was involved in the thickest of the fight. Sommacampagna was attacked; but a most strenuous resistance was offered by the Piedmontese: the Austrians, however, having been strengthened by an opportune arrival of reinforcements, the heights were retaken, but the Piedmontese still kept possession of the village most valiantly. The Austrian commander was bent on having possession of this spot, and, by reiterated charges, at length succeeded, and their enemy retreated, fighting from house to house. The Piedmontese attacked the Austrians with the utmost fury, who also returned to the charge with intrepidity; so that it became a pitched battle between the two armies, in all parts of the field.

The marshal, by his presence everywhere, animated his soldiers and huzzaed them to renewed exertion and perseverance. After the unsuccessful attack on Valeggio, General Bava in the afternoon made an attempt to take the left flank of the first corps of the Austrian army. With great resolution he advanced in this direction, and ascended the nearest heights. The Austrians did not retreat, but executed a change of front in the left flank backwards; so that, instead of being to the south, they fronted the east, and hindered by this clever manœuvre a separation between the first and second corps of the army, and spared the commander-in-chief the necessity of bringing forward his reserves. After fighting the whole day with the utmost bravery and devotion, and after making another attempt during the night upon Valeggio, with the most daring courage, the Piedmontese retreated to Custozza; and from thence to Villafranca, and afterwards to Goito. At the Piedmontese head-quarters they had depended on the co-operation of General de Sonnaz, who was, however, unable at the proper time to afford it, his troops having suffered very severely in former combats; but when he did make his appearance he attacked the Austrians fiercely, and, although no permanent good was effected, he harassed them most considerably. But in the main, the Piedmontese army, finding itself baffled, concentrated itself round Villafranca; and the retreat to the Mincio was operated at midnight, in the best order, in *echelon*.

Before daybreak next day the Austrians were off to attack the flank of the Piedmontese marching columns, and Radetzky hastened to complete his victory by an energetic pursuit of the enemy upon all points.

Soon after this, some Piedmontese heralds appeared in the Austrian camp, in order to obtain a truce. They proposed the Oglio as a demarcation line; but the marshal demanded the Adda; also Peschiera, Rizzighetto, and Rocca d'Anfo; the evacuation of Venice by the Piedmontese, as also Modena and Parma, and the enlargement of those Austrian officers detained at Milan. The king rejected these propositions, and broke up for Marcaria and Canneto on the Oglio. The marshal followed closely towards the Oglio, and sent a sufficient force to besiege Peschiera. General Bava, upon whom now had devolved the chief command of the Piedmontese army, found that the Oglio was a bad line of defence, and determined to retire farther on the Adda. The Austrians crossed the Oglio without serious molestation, and moved towards Cremona. The king wished to maintain this place, but the Austrians were too quick for him ; and before he could make his preparations they were upon him ; but, nevertheless, a most determined resistance was here made to the further advance of the Austrians, and it was supposed that another general conflict would ensue; but the experienced General Bava thought it more prudent to continue his retreat over the Adda, and Cremona surrendered to the Austrians.

The Piedmontese put every possible impediment in the way of the Austrians, but they still continued their retreat upon Piacenza, and a position upon the right shore of the Po appeared the best plan that the Piedmontese army could follow; but then the city of Milan ran the danger of being attacked by a detached Austrian corps. When this plan of operations was mentioned to the king, he interrupted the speaker, by saying,—

"No,—no. I desire that my army should hasten to the assistance of the brave Milanese, and with them fight the enemy under the city walls—the city is stored with provisions and military supplies—they have made preparations for a defence; we will complete them, and victory will turn on our side."

Thither, therefore, the army proceeded, but the gratitude of the inhabitants for this noble resolve of Charles Albert was shown in a most extraordinary manner. The Austrians, although pursuing, had still to fight their way, and many a bloody skirmish took place, as they passed along. The English minister, at the court of

Turin, now desired to negotiate a truce, but Radetzky's answer was,—"That he could accept one only on the Ticino, when he should have re-occupied all the territory belonging to his Imperial master, the Emperor."

In Milan, all was consternation and activity;—a general summons was issued by the government for all men, from the ages of eighteen and forty, to take up arms, and put themselves in motion for the Adda. The Piedmontese army had now taken up a position half a league from Milan; the right wing was leaning at Chiesa Rossa upon the canal of Pavia; the centre stood at the farms Gambaloita and Castegnedo; the left wing bent towards the Porta Orientale.

The Piedmontese soldier had naturally depended upon a hearty reception from the Milanese, but he was miserably disappointed, for he was greeted with coldness and mistrust. Partial rencontres between the two armies still continued with various local success; but still the Austrians were enabled to advance, and on the 4th of August they encamped before the gates of Milan, leaning with their right wing upon the Lambro, and the left on the canal of Pavia.

Barricades were now raised in every street in Milan, and preparations made for an obstinate resistance, and even stones were carried upon the roofs of houses in the greatest thoroughfares—but the circumstances were no longer the same as in the month of March last. After a council of war, held in the night, Charles Albert resolved to evacuate Milan, but when he acquainted the municipal authorities with the decision, and it became known in the city, loud cries of treason were heard; and the people assembling in riotous multitudes, the authorities declared that if the king did not consent to a continuation of the combat, they would not answer for his life. The king, after consideration, replied that, if the Milanese still desired war, it would be better to wage it against the enemy, than to tear each other to pieces—and the crowds seemed satisfied with this reply; but, as the king remained shut up in his palace as a hostage, and even shots were fired at the windows of his dwelling, the army was so much exasperated that it needed all the influence of their generals to prevent them from attacking the people. Whilst the king remained thus shut up, negociations for a truce continued with the Austrian commander, and, at length, an agreement was come to, according to which the Piedmontese were to leave the city early on the 6th of August, and to evacuate the Lombard territory by the 7th, in the evening—and the Austrians were to be allowed to enter Milan on the 6th, at noon.

In the night the king was claimed from

his quarters by his generals, and escorted out of the city by a detachment of troops, and the mob indemnified itself by hurrying to the various palaces and mansions of the aristocracy to plunder them. On these indications, the municipal authorities entreated the marshal to accelerate his entry into Milan, which he did (the barricades having been previously removed) at the head of the second corps of his army. A truce of six weeks was now concluded preparatory to negociations for a lasting peace—by which truce the line of demarcation between the two countries was defined—the fortresses Peschiera, Rocca d'Aufo and Osopo and the town of Brescia, were to be given up to the Austrians—the Dukedoms Modena and Parma to be entirely evacuated by the Piedmontese—and the Sardinian troops and fleet to leave Venice in order to return to Sardinia.

On the 7th of August, the veteran Radetzky thanked his brave soldiers by a special order of the day;—once more from the walls of Milan waved the Imperial banner—and no enemy remained on the Lombard territory. Soon afterwards, the Emperor issued a proclamation notifying that in the hope of seeing peace re-established in the Lombardo-Venetian kingdom shortly; and, actuated by the desire that all its people should participate in that liberty which was enjoyed by all other provinces of the Austrian empire, he declared that he had already granted to all the inhabitants, without exception, a full pardon for the part they had taken in the political events of the year, and he ordered that there should be no punishment or enquiry into any thing past—that the inhabitants of the Lombardo-Venetian kingdom should have a constitution, corresponding not only with their respective nationality and the wants of the country, but also to their union with the Austrian empire, and for that purpose, as soon as peace and tranquillity should have been restored, that he would convoke, in some place to be fixed on, the representatives of the nation, to be elected freely by all the provinces of the Lombardo-Venetian kingdom.

CHAPTER II.

Although at Vienna much ill feeling continued to be exhibited between the military and the national guard, and generally amongst the people towards each other, no serious outbreak occurred.

The Emperor came to the decision to return to his capital, which he did on the 12th of August, accompanied by his family; great preparations were made for his reception, and much cheering greeted his appearance. He proceeded at once to the cathedral of St. Stephen, and there offered up a mass for his safe return.

The workpeople and lower orders had, however, by this time, learned that they possessed a power they never dreamed of, previously to the time they had been called on by the students to raise the barricades of May, and they very soon assumed an importance and swagger, little in accordance with their appearance, but which caused much alarm in the minds of the shop-people; the journeymen would now work or not, as they pleased. If they were threatened to be discharged, they answered—"they did not care, they knew where to get money and work!" They would even bargain with their employers, as to the sort of day work they were to be employed upon, and stipulated on holidays and treats during its continuance. The government had, it was known, now declared its intention of causing the dissolution of the academic corps; and this latter body, to strengthen itself, entered again into close communion and contact with the lower orders, who, being thus supported, broke through all bounds; they traversed the city in bands, jeering and laughing at the new uniform of the national guard, and the women, in particular, openly expressed their contempt. These acts raised the ire of those would-be soldiers, who were now ever ready to make use of their arms, and many quarrels and conflicts arose in the suburbs.

The most energetic acts of the ministry of Doblhoff were the taking under its own immediate orders the disposition of the national guard, and promulgating various edicts for the restoration of order and public quiet in the city; they also issued a manifesto, dissolving the committee of public safety, the members of which, knowing what power they possessed in the new diet, separated with apparent satisfaction, giving out amongst their partisans that, as the diet was now sitting, their public functions had ceased; but they still continued, as a secret body, to watch public events, and control those acts of government which did not please them. The diet, indeed, went to work immediately, and the people were all in suspense to see what it would do. The speeches of the most radical of the members were scanned with much interest. The ministers themselves pursued a negative policy in the diet, leaving the members of the opposition to make speeches and to ask questions (which they did on all general topics of legislation, and line of policy pursued by the government), but which, if the ministers answered at all, were responded to with great reserve and reluctance. It was evident they wished to gain time to make up their minds what course should be pursued with regard to this new power, which clearly aimed at controlling the ministry in all its public acts; and which they saw was mainly composed of a very unruly, ignorant, and prejudiced set of men.

By the end of August the diet had decreed the suppression of all serfage, the total enfranchisement of the property of individuals from feudal service, and from all land-tax payable to the state; that there should not be, for the future, any difference between the immovable property of lord and peasant; that no indemnities should be accorded to the lord, excepting for the abolishment of personal serfage: in short, many rights of the landlord were abolished entirely, and every thing done to widen the breach between the lord and his peasant, by lowering the social position of the one and raising the other. Strange to say, these sudden changes were admitted by the government, and a law passed to legalize the decision of the diet in these matters.

It was known about this time that one of the most ardent and enthusiastic of the republicans of the day was in Vienna, and the effect of his presence among the lower orders was soon apparent. The *prolétaires* assumed a degree of organization that could not be mistaken. Meetings took place at the corners of streets, and in the different squares of the city, between groups of these people and persons who, singularly enough, all wore white hats. It was evident to the casual observer that the city was marching, day by day, to some important crisis; but the government appeared apathetic; no police were to be seen; the care of the property of the citizens seemed to be left to themselves; and they, forming the national guard, had now become an enormous body of men, of all conditions, quarrelling and at variance amongst themselves. Three-fourths of them were tinged with the so-called "liberal" views of the day, and the remaining portion only could be considered as staunch to the Emperor and his government. The question of the union of all Germany had more particularly divided them, and the majority hoisted the colours of united Germany, while the remainder remained true to those of Austria; so that a deadly feud arose between the "tricolor" and the "schwarz-gelb."

The different clubs held permanent sittings, where the ordinances of ministers and debates of the members of the diet were subjected to minute scrutiny. The people at large looked on the diet as the panacea for all evils, and it was their idea that the diet—and the diet alone—was the government; and the ministers, and even the Emperor himself, subordinate to its decrees. The democrats of Vienna seized every opportunity to excite and keep alive the passions of the people; and by one cause or another they succeeded in creating a species of *émeute,* or public broil, once a month. The constant arrivals of deputations from Hungary were causes of excitement to the people; and these deputations, not having their demands granted, broke out into open discontent, and harangued the people on their own supposed wrongs, inflicted by the Austrian government.

To enable the reader more readily to understand what was now passing in Vienna, we must turn to the proceedings in Hungary, and its quarrel with Croatia; for it was in consequence of this quarrel that Vienna was soon made the theatre of the most sanguinary scenes which had occurred during the year; and it was now that the Hungarians made use of the excited state of public feeling in this city to assist their own ends, by bribing the students, and through them the *prolétaires*, to pursue a line of conduct which, while it aided the Magyar party in Hungary, was made to appear to the Viennese themselves that they were only endeavouring to forward their own plans for further independence and liberty.

One of the immediate consequences of the interviews between the Emperor and the Ban of Croatia, Baron Jellacic, at Innsbruck, was an autograph letter from the former to the latter, and dated 4th September, wherein, after having extolled the fidelity and attachment of the Ban to the Imperial dynasty, and to the interests of the whole monarchy, His Majesty revoked the manifesto of the 10th of June, relating to the enquiries therein directed against the Ban, and as to his deposition from his functions.

Jellacic, being now convinced that his public conduct was approved of by the Emperor, and would receive the support of the Austrian government, lost no time in marching his troops to the frontiers between Croatia and Hungary, and in issuing a final manifesto, in which he declared that an arrogant and egotistical faction had taken advantage of the rising liberties of Hungary, to obtain concessions from the Emperor surreptitiously, which had endangered the existence of Croatia and Sclavonia—that all attempts at a mutual understanding had failed—that in vain had he attempted to insist on the inviolability of the Pragmatic Sanction, which, in its most essential clauses, adopted by the Croatian and Sclavonic nations at a diet held on the 9th of March, 1722, enacted that the kingdoms of Croatia, Sclavonia, and Dalmatia, should recognise not only the descendants, as well princes as princesses of the Imperial dynasty, a recognition which, however, was not to be acknowledged but in respect of those who should not only be in possession of Austria Proper, but also of Styria, Carniola and Carinthia, which lie within that Austria, a sanction of which the article 2, in the year 1723, stipulated expressly, and with the force of law, that the hereditary German countries, as well as the Hungarian country, should be deemed, for the purposes of government, indivisible, inseparable, and collective; that in vain had the Ban demanded a central ministry of war—of finance—of foreign affairs—and also the equality of all nationalities;—that since the Hungarian ministry at Pesth, instead of taking these peaceful arguments into consideration, had persevered in its inimical schemes, it clearly manifested its views to occasion the downfall of the monarchy, and, therefore, there was nothing more to be done than to have recourse to arms. The Ban then appealed to those Hungarian troops who did not look on the Croatians as their enemies to join him, and advised the Hungarian nation at large to seek their true enemies among those who, by cunning and fraud, had endeavoured to destroy the legal power of the crown, and had broken the ties which bound Hungary to Austria.

Crossing the frontier, and being camped now on Hungarian ground, Jellacic again addressed the natives, and declared that, on entering that country for which he felt the most lively sympathy, he called heaven to witness that he had taken that step only after all means of a friendly nature had been exhausted; and he did so, compelled by the conspiracies of a faction, of which the Hungarian ministry was only an instrument, and which, in pursuing its criminal plans, was aiming at nothing less than to degrade the Emperor, and to destroy the sacred treaty which united Hungary and its dependencies with its king and constitution; —that it was improper to declare the step which he had taken as an act of rebellion, or treason, for it had been dictated, and undertaken by him from the purest love to his country and fidelity to his king ;—that no one need apprehend that he intended to abolish a single concession or right, which had latterly been granted by the sovereign to the Hungarian nation; —that, not as an enemy, but as a friend, did he come to the aid of the loyal subjects of the constitutional king; and he therefore hoped that the Hungarian people would proffer the hand of friendship, and, with God's assistance they would deliver the country from the yoke of an incompetent, despicable, and rebellious government.

While Jellacic was thus actively employed, the Hungarian diet at Pesth wasted its time in words. A manifesto was drawn up by the ministry, addressed to the European public, and a deputation of twelve members of the diet was sent to Vienna. But every thing failed of its intended effect. Europe did not deign any answer, and the deputation returned to Pesth without having been officially received by the Emperor or the Austrian ministers.

Consternation was depicted on every man's features. In this dilemma, the whole body of ministers tendered their resignation to the Palatine, who now signified his intention of carrying on the government single handed; but in this plan he was violently opposed by the diet, who pressed Kossuth and Szemere to continue as ministers. The publication at Pesth of the Emperor's rescript in favour of Jellacic, cleared up all doubt in the minds of the Magyars, as to the determination of the Austrian government in its future conduct, and they saw that they must look to themselves alone, if they desired to continue the system so long pursued; their army was in a very disturbed state; its officers were divided amongst themselves, a large number declaring that they would not fight against their comrades the Croatians; and some of the fortresses in Hungary placed themselves under the orders of Jellacic. Indeed, there had been so much of error and misstatement, and the conduct of ministers and public men had been of so vacillating a nature, combined with the intricate line of policy pursued by Austria, that it was no wonder the generality of military men did not know which way to turn. They were threatened on all sides; they were called rebels if they adhered to the Austrian cause; they were termed deserters if they joined the Hungarians; if they fought, it was either to be against their comrades the Croatians, or their brothers in arms the Hungarians—what were they to do? In their various quarters throughout the wilds of Hungary, there was no one of whom to ask advice; the consequence was, that several attacks and contests took place in the south of Hungary, between soldiers of the same party. Such was the extreme confusion, that friends could not be distinguished from foes, or foes from friends. And now Count Louis Batthyanyi, the late president of the ministry, announced to the diet that he had received the commands of the Palatine to form a new ministry. On this being promulgated, one of the chiefs of the revolutionary party placed a hat with a huge red plume on the head of Kossuth, and invited him to harangue and stir up the people. This was done, but Kossuth's time for action had not yet arrived.

Although many names were spoken of to compose the new ministry, nothing was settled. The acting members of the government, however, made every preparation to resist the threatened invasion. A large number of the national guards at Pesth, many volunteers from Vienna, and others from the Tyrol, and those soldiers of the garrison at Buda who had been induced to desert their flag, and place themselves under that of Hungary (and there were many of them), were now sent off to the points menaced, and orders were forwarded to the different garrisons to resist the invasion of Jellacic to the uttermost. Many of the officers now saw their way more clearly, and openly left their regiments, which had declared for the Magyars, and some even carried with them the colours, and deposited them at Vienna. A part of the army of Jellacic now passed the Drave, and proceeded some way into the territory of Hungary, when he received considerable reinforcements from various regiments quartered in the vicinity of his line of march. Near St. Thomas the Magyars attacked the camp of the Raizes (Illyrians), but were signally defeated. In the midst of this warfare and confusion, the Palatine received a missive from the Emperor, which once more invited him and the Ban to settle their differences without the intervention of the sword; but it was, at the same time, hinted to the Hungarian ministry, seriously to investigate and ponder on a memorial emanating from the Austrian ministry at Vienna, which declared the existence and duration of a kingdom of Hungary, separate from the Imperial dynasty, as politically impossible, and which recommended, therefore, to the Hungarian ministry to modify its recent institutions, according to the exigencies of the Austrian government, and in conformity with the celebrated act called the Pragmatic Sanction. A meeting was accordingly proposed between Jellacic and the Palatine, and the place actually appointed ; but the fears and jealousies of parties frustrated the plan ; it was reported on either side that the meeting was merely a trap for one party to gain possession of the other, and so further their own ends ; and this seemed so probable, that all idea of it was soon given up.

Count Batthyanyi, seeing the desperate state of affairs, now declared in the diet that he had ceased to belong to the ministry; but Kossuth and others of the revolutionary party still yet induced him to remain; and the diet passing a vote of confidence in him, he consented, but on the condition that the diet should uphold his line of policy—and he declared this to be, "in disputing every inch of Hungarian ground with Jellacic." This bold commencement was received with deafening applause by the whole assembly, and the next day he communicated to the diet the names of his proposed new ministry; thus was he committed to a line of conduct diametrically opposed to the Austrian government. Kossuth, in the meanwhile, was not idle; events were ripening fast, and he knew that his turn for action was arriving with giant strides. The energy of his character now shone forcibly; he called an appeal to arms of the whole population, and proclaimed a levy *en masse*, and departed to the country, vowing that he would not return but at the head of one hundred and fifty thousand men!

Successive deputations were sent from Pesth to Vienna, and a solemn audience was claimed by the Magyars of the Emperor, who granted it—but who received their petition and complaints with the utmost coldness; one of the deputations was accredited to the diet at Vienna, which body, however, decided that it had no power to receive it. The Magyars, seeing themselves foiled on all sides, returned to Hungary, vowing vengeance and revenge. The Palatine of Hungary, the Archduke Stephen, having been called on by the Hungarian ministers to place himself at the head of the troops, professed to accept the command, but the moment that he found himself outside the city walls of Pesth, he flew to Vienna, and there laid down his onerous dignity.

A proclamation from the Austrian ministry was now published, addressed to the people of Hungary and to the troops stationed in that country; and it stated that the maintenance of the power of the Emperor was the sole means of conciliating and uniting all nationalities, which were in arms against each other; that the Emperor disapproved of the intrigues of the Hungarian ministry, and reproached them with various illegal acts, but still it was hoped that they would maintain tranquillity and peace; and concluded by commanding all persons to wait for the measures the Emperor would immediately take for the pacification of the whole country.

In the mean time Jellacic, at the same period that he was marching into the heart of Hungary, put himself in communication with the Austrian government; and not only was an imperial commissioner sent to his quarters, to aid in the progress of the plan to put down the Magyar movement, but a correspondence was entered into between Jellacic and Count Latour, the minister of war at Vienna. Part of this correspondence was intercepted, and sent to the influential democratic members of the diet of that capital, and they publicly charged the minister with sending money and arms to Jellacic, for the express purpose of subjugating the Hungarians; and, although Count Latour explained the circumstance to the complete satisfaction of the diet, this fact was laid hold of by the democrats to excite the people most violently against the line of conduct pursued by the government. A manifesto of the Emperor, as King of Hungary, was now promulgated; and by which Count François Lamberg was charged with the chief command of all the troops in Hungary, and nominated as royal commissioner to restore order and peace. It declared that the insurrection in Hungary should be put down by military force, and that all necessary measures should be taken by the Count to effectuate a satisfactory reconciliation in all parts of the kingdom.

The Hungarian diet treated this manifesto as a direct infringement of the constitution, and Kossuth, who had entered the assembly with a sword buckled to his side, declared that to be his opinion; and the diet passed a resolution that, as this ordonnance did not bear the signature of a Hungarian minister, it was, according to the fundamental laws of the country, illegal and of no effect; and that Count Lamberg, in acting under its provisions, would render himself liable to the penalties attached to those who should endanger the liberties of the nation. It further declared that Hungary owed obedience only to the president of the ministers, and to the committee of public defence! This decision of the diet was published throughout Pesth on the morning of the 20th of September, and raised an extraordinary excitement among the people.

About one o'clock in the day a band of Magyars appeared at the guard-house of the bridge crossing the Danube, and demanded a drum to beat an alarm, for Count Lamberg, said they, had arrived at Buda; and they were prepared to seize him and hang him up. They cried out that he was at the hotel of Count Hrabowsky. A crowd soon assembled, and gave themselves up to violence, and all started off for the habitation of Count Hrabowsky. They burst open the gates and rushed through the apartments, breaking the windows and furniture of the rooms. As soon as Count Hrabowsky appeared on the first floor, he was seized, and held prisoner in an inner room, but Count Lamberg was not to be found. He had escaped by a back door, and had hastened to cross the bridge in a carriage, to Pesth, to put himself under the protection of the diet. In the middle of the bridge, a number of national guards, and men armed with scythes, were posted. The Count was immediately recognized, and dragged out of the vehicle. A man stepped forward and cried out, "Who are you?" The Count answered—"The royal commissioner, Count Lamberg."—"Go to hell, then," was the answer of the brute, while striking him heavily on the head.

A scene now ensued difficult to describe. The mob seized the half dead and bleeding body of the Count, and dragged it along the remaining length of the bridge into the city of Pesth. They then pierced it with a hundred bayonets. They cut off his legs and arms with their scythes, and raised the body on the points of their weapons, rushing through the streets with it like so many devils. The ensuing scene was truly indescribable; and although the diet declared that they disapproved the act, and instigated an enquiry to ascertain the murderers, no one was arrested, and after a short time all enquiry respecting the matter ceased. Count Louis Batthyanyi, immediately after this horrid murder, made his escape from Pesth.

It became now highly necessary for the Austrian ministry to take decided steps; and on the 3rd of October appeared a proclamation, in due form, with the Emperor's signature, and also that of Adam Recsci, the then president of the Hungarian ministry, and who had been appointed by the Emperor. This proclamation was addressed to the barons, ecclesiastical and civil dignitaries, magnates, and deputies, assembled in the diet convoked by the king at Pesth; and after stating that the members of the diet of Hungary had been led away by Kossuth and his partizans to great illegalities, which had caused the Emperor the deepest sorrow and indignation; that the diet had put in execution several illegal resolutions against the royal will, and had latterly carried a vote against the mission of the royal commissoner,

Count Lamberg, sent by him to establish peace; in consequence of which he had been furiously assaulted in the public streets by a wild mob, and most frightfully murdered, the Emperor notified that he felt obliged, under the circumstances, and in accordance with his royal duty for maintaining the public safety, and the laws of the country, to enact the following decrees and to command their execution. 1st. He thereby dissolved the diet, which was to close its session instantaneously. 2nd. He declared all resolutions and measures of that diet, which had not been sanctioned by him, to be illegal, null, and without any efficiency. 3rd. He placed all the troops and armed corps, stationed in Hungary and its dependencies and in Transylvania, be they of what description soever, militia or volunteers, under the command of the Ban of Croatia, Baron Jellacic. 4th. That the kingdom of Hungary was placed under martial law, till the period when the peace of the country should be re-established; and the assemblies of the congregations of the country towns and districts were interdicted. 5th. That the Ban of Croatia was thereby sent as plenipotent commissary, invested with full power and authority to exercise, in the sphere of the executive, those rights, in the possession of which he had been placed, in the present extraordinary circumstances, as substitute of the Emperor. 6th. That Baron Jellacic should particularly take care that the assaulters and murderers of Count Lamberg, as well as all the movers and participators in that shameless crime, should be proceeded against with all the severity of the law. And, 7th. That the administration of all civil affairs would be carried on, in the meanwhile, according to law, by the functionaries employed in the respective ministries; and all necessary measures to guard and administer the common interests of the whole monarchy on a permanent basis; and to guarantee, for ever, equality of rights to all nationalities, and to settle upon this foundation the mutual relations of all the countries and peoples united under the imperial dynasty, should be deliberated upon with the consent and concurrence of the representatives from all parts, and determined in due legal form.

Tumultuous meetings of the democrats of Vienna now took place at the Odeon, on the 3rd, 4th, and 5th October. The most violent speeches and invectives against the government were indulged in, and it was then resolved that the time was come to carry into execution their long cherished plan of creating an *émeute* on a grand scale, which, while it might further their own general revolutionary views, should assist the Magyar movement in Hungary, by diverting the attention of the government from what was passing in that country.

It was asserted throughout Vienna, that

as much as six hundred thousand florins (sixty thousand pounds) had been during these days deposited in the hands of the chiefs of the democrats, to be by them distributed amongst the population and military stationed there; and it was openly reported that threats had been used at those meetings, not only against the life of the Minister of War, Count Latour, but also against those of some other of the ministers, and that of the Emperor himself. The government was well acquainted with all that had passed, but, by a strange infatuation, thought itself sufficiently strong to put down and repel any aggression.

In this state of affairs arrived the morning of the 6th October, a day memorable in the annals of Austria. On this morning, a battalion of German grenadiers from the regiments "Hess," "Baden," and "Hrabowsky," and a battalion of the Italian grenadiers, had received orders to march towards Hungary.

As these battalions showed some unwillingness to obey the orders given (for they had been tampered with by the democrats), a strong detachment of cuirassiers was commanded to escort them to the railroad station; but an immense number of the national guard and academic legion had already assembled and encouraged the troops in their disobedience of orders, and some thousands of the lower orders of the people, with women and children, congregated at the railroad station in the court-yard, and there they by force tore up the rails to prevent the departure of the troops. This difficulty was met by the authorities, with an order that the troops should march to the first station, about five miles distant. The people, on hearing this, rushed to the bridge called the Tabor bridge, which crossed a branch of the Danube, over which the soldiers had to pass, and destroyed it, so that the military were again hindered from starting. The mob also destroyed another bridge further on, over the same branch of the river, and pulled down the telegraph. The country-people from the numerous surrounding districts joined the work-people of the city, and they, with the national guards and academic legion, and the rest of the students, now formed one dense mob near and about the railway station, and they shouted that the troops should not go to Hungary. The refractory military, of course, took advantage of every expedient thrown in the way by the people, and still hesitated to proceed. But now, a heavy detachment of the Polish regiment "Nassau" approached the scene of disorder with four pieces of cannon; but on the first order for the refractory troops to advance, they flatly refused to move. This was the signal for the outbreak. Some of the members of the diet, who had mixed with the crowd, and in fact aided the movement, declared to the people that they would immediately go and demand that the order for the military to march to Hungary should be rescinded. But already had the grenadiers mixed themselves with the people, so that all military discipline had disappeared among them, and a vast mob, with them in their centre, began to return to the city. At this period a detachment of sappers arrived, and began to restore the first broken bridge. Suddenly, a number of the people rushed on the four cannon belonging to the Nassau regiment, and got possession of three out of the four, together with a quantity of ammunition. The Nassau regiment immediately fired a volley on the people, and many of them fell. This was the first bloodshed on this memorable day, and it appeared to be the signal for a deadly conflict. On either side volleys were fired, and the people, aided by the refractory regiments, employed the cannon taken against their adversaries. A general and a major commanding the troops fell, and after a heavy firing the regiment retired. This was a moment of extreme exultation to the people, who now shouted that they had gained the day; and the whole mass of people, national guard, academic corps, students, women and children, to the number of seventy or eighty thousand, returned to the city, bearing with them the three cannon and the hat of the slain general, which they hoisted as a trophy. Within the city walls, in the meantime, the efforts of the insurgents had been well seconded. A portion of the national guard beat an alarm through the principal streets, and amassed as many of their followers as they could; and they formed themselves into line in the different public squares and streets.

Towards twelve o'clock, the baggage of the troops who had been ordered to Hungary was seen slowly returning towards the city, and the people seemed to have gained the day. But the public rancour against the military increased each moment; and if any soldiers were perceived, they were immediately chased, hooted at, and fired on. A party of cuirassiers, who still hovered near the returning mob, approached the inner city by the suburb called the Leopoldstadt; but the people halted at the end of this street, and pointed the three cannon in their possession at them, and this made the cuirassiers turn down another street. Here, however, they were met by a large body of the national guard, who refused to let them pass. The cuirassiers rushed on to make a passage through them, but a well-directed discharge of musketry killed and wounded several, and threw them into confusion, and they dispersed to make their way separately as best they could. This again caused great exultation to the people, who began to think their party invincible. There was no longer any enemy without the walls, and every one rushed onward into the city.

Whilst all this was passing, the students and democratic clubs' committee was assembled, and held constant communication with the people, who appeared to be well disciplined and under orders. The diet assembled late in the day, for the president refused to open the sittings at the usual time. About one o'clock the national guards of the suburb called the Wieden (and which was always considered the most democratic suburb of Vienna) arrived at the place of Saint Stephen, near the Cathedral. The national guard of the Kärnthner quarter (and who adhered to their duty, and were consequently detested by the people,) were on duty round this edifice, and on some gross provocation being given, they fired at their Wieden brethren. This was instantaneously returned by the latter, and at the same moment, from the windows of various houses in the immediate neighbourhood, firing began against the devoted Kärnthner quarter guard, and they were forced quickly to retire, leaving many of their comrades on the pavement dead.

The ministry, on being made acquainted with this fatal rencounter, at length roused itself, and issued a proclamation, which was soon posted up, headed, "To the National Guards;" and it stated that they had heard with extreme regret, that one part of the national guard was fighting against the other; that citizens fired on citizens without the least reason for doing so; that anarchy could only ensue from such conduct; that the ministry was firmly resolved to keep peace, order, and liberty, and by that proclamation summoned such of the national guard who would support them, to make themselves known by wearing a white ribbon round the arm! Thus were they wasting their time in words, when the period for action had almost passed away! This order proved most injudicious, for the poor national guards who remained faithful, became at once a mark for the people to fire at.

About two o'clock, several companies of sappers and miners, accompanied by two pieces of artillery, came rushing along the streets, and flew down the Graben towards the Saint Stephen's Place; and it was here that they met the victorious mob returning from the railroad station. These, then, with the guard of the Wieden suburb, received this body of military with savage shouts, and, rushing on and firing at them, caused them to retire quickly. They retreated, firing all the way along the Graben, and they themselves were also fired at by insurgents from the windows on either side of this street, and quickly pursued by the mob. They were enabled, however, to point their two cannon against the people at the end of the Graben, and discharged them, but the shot struck too high. The people rushed with impetuous fury on the cannon, seized them, and killed the commanding officer and many of the men, and forced the remainder still to continue their retreat through the streets. And now, at the lower end of the city, near the university (through which quarter the people had penetrated victoriously), barricades were raised, which increased in number in each street in an incredible short space of time, so that, as the people fought their way through the streets, barricades rose behind them, formed by thousands of workmen with tools of every description for that purpose.

And now the principal part of the mob had reached the public square called the Hof; and there were six cannon in possession of the guard at the war office situated in this square. The artillery-men, as the crowd was pressing through the narrow street leading to the Hof, pointed three of the cannon against them, and discharged them; but instead of attempting to hold their position, they immediately turned with their cannon into the court-yard of the war-office, and closed the outer gates. The company of soldiers on guard formed in front and at the side of this building; but before they received any orders to act, they were assailed by musket shots from the windows of each story of almost every house near them—the people, shouting and vociferating, poured into the square, and were on them instantly — firing continued on all sides, and a number of soldiers fell. The remainder, seeing themselves assailed on all sides, and receiving no orders what to do, poured in a volley amongst the people and retreated as best they might. They were followed closely by the mob, and the appearance of the square was like that of a chase. The people took deliberate aim, and shot the troops down without mercy. They retreated across the wide space; and then, dividing themselves into two parties, (one bearing across the Freyung towards the city gate called the Schotten, the other turning off to the left to seek another gate not far off,) they escaped. They were followed quickly by the mob, who fired continually on them, causing great execution, and they were assisted by murderous discharges from the windows of the houses on either side of the streets. Thus the military were turned out of the city, and the gates closed upon them. And now the Hof was filled by thousands of the national guard, the academic legion, the students, and ruffians of all kinds, armed with crow-bars, scythes, pitchforks, spades and axes, who shouted frantically for the Minister of War, Count Latour. He was indeed at the war-office, holding council with Back and other of the ministers. These latter, perceiving the victory the insurgents had obtained, at once made their escape by a side gateway. But not so the poor Minister of War. In a little time the gates were forced; the mob rushed on the few remaining artillery-men and guards within the court, and seized the pieces of cannon.

In the meantime the diet had voted itself in permanence, and had passed a decree, taking the ministry under its protection, and had sent two of their deputies to the war-office to defend Count Latour from the rage of the populace. This was at four o'clock in the afternoon; and now the ill-fated minister appeared on the staircase, escorted by the two deputies. These persons made known the mandate of the diet; but during the furious intoxication of the people, who would listen to anything!—they cried out savagely that they would have the life of the minister. About twenty of the principal of the national guard and academic corps gave their word of honour that they would guard the minister in safety; but at this moment a body of men of the lowest class, armed with crow-bars and hammers, rushed towards the minister and those near him; the first blow from a hammer was parried by one of the deputies, but Latour was assailed on all sides. He had but time to say—"I have a clear conscience before God—I die innocent!" when he was struck down by a blacksmith with an iron crow-bar, and instantly murdered in cold blood by these infuriated demons. The two deputies made their escape, and returned to the diet to report the scene The villains then hung up the body of the minister, still reeking in blood and in the convulsive agonies of death, to the lamp-post in the court-yard; but a cry of "Bring him out!" caused them to take him down, and they trailed the body out of the court-yard into the Hof, to a gas lamp opposite the war-office, in front of the minister's own windows; a ladder was procured and fixed against the lamp-post, and a man in a blouse ascended, dragging the body of the murdered man after him, and he attempted to fix it to the lamp-post; the rope, however, was not sufficiently long, and he let the body fall to the ground. A soldier ungirt his leather waistband, and having fixed the body to it, handed up the other end, which was passed over one of the three projecting irons of the lamp-post, and the body was again hoisted in the air. The corpse was thus hung up; the clothes were torn from the body, and it was then subjected to every indignity the most depraved imagination could think of; the miscreants kept swinging the body to and fro, shouting frantically; and, after a time, about fifty musket-shots were fired at it by the surrounding devils. An immense crowd collected in this locality until late at night, occupied in acts of the most ferocious joy. At two in the morning, the Hof was vacated by these infuriated beings; and a sheet having been procured, some one ascended the ladder, and taking down the body, carried it away.

An address was now voted by the diet to the Emperor, in which it demanded a popular ministry, with two of the ministers, named Hornbostl and Doblhoff, at its head; the instant dismissal of Jellacic from the post of commissioner of Hungary, and an amnesty for every one, both civil and military, concerned in the day's "transactions;" and these ministers set off for Shöenbrunn, where the Emperor was residing, accompanied by some of the principal members on the opposition side of the diet. A placard appeared on all the walls of the city announcing that the diet remained in permanence to consult on the best measures to cause the total evacuation of the city, by the military, and to obtain a general amnesty for those engaged in the "accidents" of the day. It was now night, and the people were complete masters of the city; they rushed through the streets shouting for arms, although bearing hatchets, crow-bars, and scythes, and precipitated themselves towards the military arsenal, in the street called the Renn Gasse; but this building was still occupied by a strong body of military, consisting of those who were on guard, and such of the soldiers who were able to seek a refuge from the multitude, and a large number of the national guard, still remaining true to their colours. As the mob approached, they were received by a well-directed volley from the arsenal, and forced to retreat, leaving many of their comrades dead in the street; but they soon returned to the charge, and a sanguinary battle now took place at this spot between the two parties, the students and national guard leading on the mob; these last brought forward one of the cannon lately captured, and at one discharge burst open the door of the arsenal. They then rushed on to storm the place; but the troops within had prepared two obuses, which they had planted at the opening, and applying the match, they caused a horrid carnage among the people, who, seeing so many of their comrades fall, retired in great disorder to some distance; the troops now barricaded their gate, and the mob on their side formed a huge barricade in the street at a little way opposite the gate of the arsenal, from behind which they continued firing musket-balls at the building; these had, however, but little effect, as the whole edifice was bomb-proof. The combat ceased for some time; for commissioners from the diet now arrived bearing orders from that body to the defenders of the arsenal to lay down their arms; but it was soon reported to these commissioners, that whoever approached the gate would be instantly shot.

And now, to add to the general confusion, a report was spread through the city, that reinforcements of military had arrived by the railroad from Wiener Neustadt, and that vengeance would be taken for the occurrences of the day. The diet published a manifesto, forbidding the directors of the railway to allow any military to be thus transported. Many of the deputies, seeing how matters were likely to turn, openly left the diet, and made their escape from the city. The remainder, who consisted chiefly of the opposition, vowed to remain, as they said, "to protect the state."

Quite late in the evening, a paper was drawn up by the central committee of the democratic clubs, and presented to the committee of safety, which had been nominated by the diet, demanding that the diet should address his majesty to obtain the withdrawal of the military order of the 5th of October for the marching of the troops to Hungary;—the express acknowledgment of the sovereignty of the constitutional diet, headed by Kossuth, in Hungary;—the immediate re-establishment of peace between the Hungarians and the

Croatians on the basis of the equality of all nationalities, and the reinstatement of all the constitutional rights of Hungary ;—that all irresponsible ministers should be dismissed ;—to dissolve the present ministry, and to compose one in a more liberal sense ;—to declare that thenceforward the ministry should be responsible for its acts ;—that the minister of war should only garrison Vienna with troops well affected towards the inhabitants, and that the military should be placed in absolute submission to the civil authorities ;—that a complete amnesty should be granted to those troops who had taken part with the people : and that the city of Vienna should not be placed in a state of siege.

During all this time the attacks on the military arsenal continued ; but, notwithstanding that cannon had been placed nearly all round the edifice, and that huge flakes of fire had been thrown into it, not the slightest perceptible impression was made, excepting on the outer walls, which showed the marks of the balls. About midnight the deputation, with the above requisitions, returned from Shöenbrunn, with the account that they had seen the Emperor, who had consented to appoint a popular ministry without delay.

The noise and confusion continued the whole night within the city walls; and the most horrible disorder was prevalent; without, the military was posted on the glacis, and remained under arms, ready to act on the first signal. Early on the morning of the seventh of October, the troops and national guard in the arsenal received orders to retire, which they did by secret paths under ground leading to the glacis; and the building was then occupied by its assailants, who seized on all the arms they could find. After the arsenal had been well ransacked, the diet issued an order that arms were not to be carried away from the arsenal—that the gates should be closed, and no one was to enter except on material business! During this day, and in the evening, the military, to the amount of between eight or nine thousand men, retired from the glacis, and took up a position in the garden of Prince Schwarzenberg, which commanded the city. And now it was announced that the Emperor and the whole Imperial family had quitted Shöenbrunn, taking with them two thousand of the troops as a guard. This news caused the greatest consternation. The finance minister Kraus announced to the diet that he had received a sealed dispatch from the Emperor, which contained a manifesto, and he was directed to countersign it and make it public. This manifesto was in the following words:—

"I have endeavoured to fulfil all the wishes of my people—every thing that could conduce to the happiness and well-being of the community have I done willingly; and I have now lately granted them a constitution. Although the events of May drove me from the palace of my ancestors, I did not hesitate to grant what my people desired; the diet was formed and convoked on the most liberal basis. I returned to my capital without seeking any other guarantee than the loyalty and gratitude of my people; but a small number of malcontents menace all the friends of the country with destruction. Vienna is filled with fire and blood; my minister of war, whose advanced age should have saved him, has expired under the hands of murderous wretches. I confide in God and in my just rights, and quit my capital to seek the means of sending succour to my subjugated people. Let all those who love Austria and true liberty, range themselves round their Emperor."

The Imperial family took the road to Saint Pölten, crossed the Danube by the bridge of that town, and sought shelter in the fortress of Olmutz.

The diet, now finding itself freed from all restraint, assumed all the powers of the state; and the people looked up to it as the only governing power.

CHAPTER III.

It may be readily imagined what would be the conduct of the revolutionary portion of the diet in Hungary, and of the brutal populace of Pesth, on the reception and promulgation of the edict of the Emperor, their king, of the 3rd of October.

During the last days of September the greatest consternation had continued to reign in the city; the national guard, ever since the day of the murder of Count

Lamberg, had received orders not to assemble themselves, or to exercise in public—the most distinguished families had fled—the respectable part of the diet had retired from their posts in disgust; and the greater part of the population were preparing to follow these examples, when the diet (or that revolutionary portion of it which arrogated to itself the powers of that body) issued an order to suspend the sailing of the steamers and all other vessels in the Danube; and an organization of the levy *en masse* was ordered.

By the time that the news of the insurrection at Vienna of the 6th of October reached Pesth, public agitation was at its height. Nothing now remained for the democratic party but to draw the sword and throw away the scabbard, or to submit unconditionally to the Emperor's decree.

On the 8th of October, the diet, on the proposition of one of the most active of its revolutionary members, nominated Kossuth as President of the Committee of Defence. This enterprising man had lately returned from his tour in the provinces, in the vicinity of the Theiss, where he had been, as he truly said, to organize the rising of the Landsturm; and he now reported that the Hungarian lion, so long asleep, had at last awoke, that the organization was complete, and the people ready to obey the call of the country for its defence.

Kossuth now found himself, flung by the force of events at the summit of power; he had long desired to take steps which should make a retreat from revolution impracticable, and which would deliver the fate of the country into his hands; and now this long-desired object was accomplished, and he made a masterly use of the occasion.

In the position of President of the Committee of Defence, he developed all his talent for agitation, all his powers to conciliate and to inflame. It is impossible to deny the vast ability he showed for the carrying out his ambitious plans, and the course of events aided him considerably. The anticipated evacuation of the Hungarian soil by Jellacic encouraged the wildest hopes of the insurgents, and the great development of force from all parts of the country to the standard of Kossuth excited universal astonishment. The question as to how this vast army should be maintained vanished, on the fact being known that, by means of the government bank-note press, he was enabled to coin money, and the promulgation of a decree of the diet to make it pass current, proclaiming death to all who should refuse to accept it as the current coin of the realm.

The aristocracy of Hungary, with some exceptions, held itself aloof, and preserved a taciturn neutrality. The Palatine had fled to Vienna; Count Batthyanyi had also retired, astounded and scared by the bold measures of Kossuth. The new President of the diet appointed by them had also abandoned his post and joined the Magyar army. The members of the Committee of Defence upheld Kossuth in all his views, for at the first sitting of this body after his election as President he assumed all superiority, and assigned to each member his separate sphere of action; the diet had become his willing slave, and the whole revolutionary party now looked upon him as their head and chief. A distinguished Magyar, of the name of Moga had been chosen as general of the insurrectionary army, and he now set out in search of Jellacic; it had already been reported that this latter, with his Croatians, was traversing Hungary, with a view to reach the Austrian capital; and, indeed, during his passage, he had sustained some heavy reverses from a portion of the Magyar army stationed in the various parts of the country through which he had to pass. Jellacic had determined to transfer his head-quarters in the first instance to Veleneze, but on his way thither he fell in with the Magyar army under Moga; a battle ensued, which continued from nine in the morning until six at night. Each party claimed the victory; the Magyars, because they had maintained their position during the day, the Croatians, because Moga retreated the next day to within twenty miles of Pesth, and from the fact that he sent to Jellacic, and concluded with him a truce for three days. Jellacic employed this time in marching on towards Vienna, where he suspected his services might soon be required. At the end of the truce Moga cautiously followed the Croatian army, until he had ascertained that it was no longer on Hungarian soil; he indeed crossed the frontier into Austria, but quickly retreated to his own country.

Notwithstanding it was now known at Pesth that Jellacic had evacuated Hungary, the panic continued; and it was raised to its highest pitch by the appearance of a placard, notifying that Count Oden Zichy, late administrator of the comitat of Stahlweissenberg, had been hung, in pursuance of the sentence of a court-martial, for having betrayed his country in allying himself with the Croatians, its deadly enemies. This deed was committed under the direction of Major Arthur Georgey, and it was now that the name of this celebrated person first became notorious. The iron severity of the Major drew Kossuth's attention towards him, and he soon after became the chief favourite of the agitator.

This celebrated person was born in the county of Zips, in Hungary, in the year 1818, of a good family. He received from his mother the education of a Spartan; the philosophy of her affection consisted in enuring him, when a child, to all sorts of hardships; at the age of fourteen he entered the college at Eperies, and thence proceeded to the Imperial school at Saln, where he much distinguished himself by his application and talents. On leaving this establishment he entered the Hungarian noble guard at Vienna, and a few years afterwards received his commission as lieutenant in the Imperial Palatinate hussars. In this regiment he did not, however, serve long; the inactive life, and the prospect of slow advancement, were the prominent motives of his quitting the army. After taking this step he retired to Prague, where he devoted himself to the study of chemistry, in which he made great progress. At Prague he became acquainted with a French lady, who was governess in a family, and very highly respected and beloved, and whom he afterwards married. On the revolutionary movement breaking out in 1848 he returned to his native country, and offered his services to the Hungarian provisional government; they were accepted, and he was appointed major in a regiment of hussars, which formed part of the army then operating against the Ban Jellacic. Georgey's personal appearance is striking, though not prepoesessing; his features express sternness and severity; he is of fine manly stature, muscular, broad-shouldered and tall, with fair hair, intelligent forehead, blue eyes, aquiline nose, and much firmness about the mouth. His character is brave, ambitious, and, as a general, severe, but towards his prisoners courteous and *chevaleresque.* In private life he is mild and cheerful; his favourite themes of conversation are chemistry and medicine; but on political subjects he is very reserved.

The fortresses of Comorn, Esseg, Peterwardein, Munkrac and Leopoldstadt had opened their gates to the Magyars, and each had received a considerable garrison; two fortresses only, Arad and Temeswar, scorning to imitate such examples, remained true to their oath and their sovereign.

Various conflicts continued to take place in different parts of Servia and Hungary; but public attention was now fixed on the principal events taking place at Vienna, and on the frontiers of Austria and Hungary, where the army of Moga was in position.

The portion of the diet still remaining at Vienna now issued its proclamations, decrees, and orders, on all subjects connected with the city; and, amongst others, it declared itself in permanence, named a committee to maintain public order; announced to the public that the ministers, Doblhoff, Hornbostl, and Kraus would, for the future, direct all public affairs; that it would soon present a list of the intended new ministry to his majesty; and that it (the diet) would send a thank-offering to the Emperor, to convince him of the unalterable love and fidelity of his people! The diet, moreover, declared that it would not dissolve itself, that it was an indivisible totality, and that it represented all the people of Austria who had sent deputies; that in consequence of the Imperial manifesto of the 6th of June, and of the free choice of the people, it was the sole constitutional legal organ of union between the constitutional monarch and the sovereignty of the people, for the guarantee of liberty and the hereditary throne; that it would not impose the moral obligation on any deputy of remaining a member against his will, but that all absent deputies must return to the chambers within fifteen days from the publication of that resolution. These latter clauses were levelled against a large number of the diet who had quitted Vienna, and taken refuge at Prague, and who had publicly declared that the insurrection at Vienna was the work of strangers—that it was criminal; for, by violence and murder, it had succeeded in overturning a ministry which possessed the confidence of the diet; and they protested against all the decrees emanating from that portion of the diet still sitting at Vienna.

It was now reported at Vienna that Jellacic had crossed the Austrian frontier from Hungary with a numerous army, and was on his way to the capital, to join the military stationed in the Schwarzenberg gardens, under the command of Count Auersberg. The diet dispatched a deputy to ascertain the truth; and, in fact, he found him at the castle of Schwadorf, surrounded by his officers and troops. The Ban declared to him that he could take no notice of the diet of Austria in any matter relating to Hungary, but only on the affairs of the whole monarchy, whose interest he was bound to support—that his sole desire was to conduct his army to the assistance of the Emperor; and that he could only receive orders from his Majesty himself.

The first act of the Emperor, after his arrival at Olmütz, was the publication of a manifesto, wherein he declared that he found himself obliged to oppose force not only to the insurrection at Vienna, but also to other parts of his dominions, until order, tranquillity, and obedience to the laws, should be re-established, and the assassins of Counts Lamberg and Latour brought to justice; that he thereby invested Prince Windishgrätz with the supreme command of all the troops of the empire, with the exception of those in Italy; and he further notified that the events of the 6th of October had obliged him to transfer, temporarily, his residence to Olmütz; that all liberties and rights which had been conceded to his people would be upheld, and that he would continue the work of the constitution, which had already made some progress. The Emperor also addressed the people of Hungary, Croatia, Sclavonia, Transylvania, and the military borders. He stated that his aim was to insure the full enjoyment of liberty to his people, with the blessings of peace and order, which had been so much disturbed by the treacherous agitations of a faction; that he would never tolerate the oppressions of any one nationality over another; that he would realize the equality of rights for each nation, on the basis of the constitutitional laws of the countries annexed to the kingdom of Hungary; that all concessions granted to the peasants, in their relations with their lords, should be upheld, and exhorted all those who loved their country and the reigning dynasty to rally round his standard. Immediately after the promulgation of these decrees, Prince Windishgrätz took the chief command of the Austrian armies, and at once declared the city of Vienna in a state of siege.

The inhabitants were now terribly alarmed, and began to quit the city in great numbers; and by the middle of the month of October more than sixty thousand persons had fled. The *prolétériat* had been by this time drilled, and they marched through the city in bands of one hundred each; but their appearance was squalid and miserable in the extreme. At the head of each band was a student, in a state of exaltation. He seemed to himself to be at the pinnacle of glory; and with his Calabrian hat cocked on one side, his long black feather dangling, his dingy hair floating on his shoulders, his broad leather belt drawn tightly round his waist and garnished with pistols, and with his sword drawn, he marched with his cadaverous comrades through the city, as if in triumph; little imagining the pitiful figure he made in the eyes of the few respectable persons who yet remained in Vienna!

The diet now began to mistrust its own friends, and, for the safety of the city, it decreed that all public buildings should be under its special protection; and printed notices to this effect were posted on all the government and public edifices. A number of the National Guard was sent to each member of the diplomatic corps, as a protection to their premises. Their whole duty, however, consisted in eating and drinking, and marching to and fro, before the door; presenting arms to every one who passed, and everlastingly smoking their meerschaums: they at once declared that they had no power or control over the *proltéaires*, if they chose to act.

The shopkeepers now inscribed on their shutters the motto, — "That property was to be held sacred;"—but they lived, from day to day, in the fear of robbery and spoliation. In the evening, in the streets were to be seen knots of ferocious-looking fellows, armed to the teeth.

The fires burned vividly behind the barricades, around which were seated men in blouses, students and women of the lowest class, some groups playing at cards or dice, others lying full-length on the straw; all half drunk, noisy, and quarrelsome. The cannon were posted on the bastions, the *mèches* were kept lighted, and men of all grades lounged about near them; the National Guard, a part of the city artillery corps, the military who had deserted, the Academic Legion with their Calabrian hats and stolen arms, work-people in their short sleeves and bare brawny arms, all made motley groups; and they patrolled the city, accompanied by the noise of a broken or loosely strung-up drum, armed with old muskets without flints or bayonets, carbines, lances, and even Turkish scymetars, all stolen from the arsenal.

The diet, not comprehending the inactivity of the military outside the city, and becoming terribly alarmed at the signs within, sent another agent to Jellacic, to endeavour to ascertain his intentions, who brought back the following written declaration from that General:—"The reasons which induce me to order my troops to their present position, concern me only as officer of the state and as a soldier. As officer of the state, I obey the commands of my Emperor, and endeavour to put down anarchy. As soldier, the sound of cannon indicates the road I shall take. I am not pursued by the Hungarians, as you suppose; but, should they dare to pass the Austrian frontier, I shall march against them as enemies to my country. My troops pay for all they receive; they encamp in the open air. On the Austrian territory I know no difference between Hungarian and Croatian troops; I acknowledge them only as Austrian soldiers."

Notwithstanding this candid declaration,

Messenhauser, the commander of the national guard at Vienna, lately appointed to that post by the diet, notified to the inhabitants that the Hungarian army, under the command of Moga, had passed the frontiers, and had made preparations to encamp near Vienna, and had confided the superior command of their troops to General Bem.

General Bem had been, indeed, induced to join the Hungarian insurrection, and had then lately arrived in Vienna to take the direction of affairs there, in order to further the interests of the revolution in Hungary. This celebrated person was born at Tarnou, in Gallicia, in the year 1795; he studied at Cracow, and afterwards was placed in the military school at Warsaw; he was lieutenant of artillery in 1812, and served against Russia in the campaign of that year; in 1819 he was named captain under the Grand Duke Constantine, in the newly-organised Polish army, but, having been suspected of revolutionary tendencies, he was cited before a military tribunal in 1825, and lost his grade in the army. He then applied himself to mechanical sciences. After the revolt of Warsaw, in 1830, he obtained a command in the insurrectionary army, and distinguished himself in many of the conflicts; he was rapidly advanced to the grade of colonel, and then promoted to the chief command of the artillery. The insurrection was, however, put down by Russia, and Bem retired to France.

Since that time he had supported himself by literary productions and efforts of mechanical skill. He was brave even to audacity, and had received many wounds. At the time of his appearance at Vienna he was in a bad state of health, and it required a long time each day to bandage his wounds, so as to enable him to appear in public, notwithstanding which, his energies were undaunted, and his activity wonderful. His personal appearance at this time was of the middle height; he was thin, but had a round face, with a brown and ruddy complexion, low forehead, hair mixed with grey, grey eyebrows, nose pointed and aquiline, a broad mouth, and a moustache; he held conversation in Polish, French, and German, and had the appearance of a clever, gentlemanly officer.

And now all the inhabitants of Vienna were summoned to take arms; and a motley crew indeed responded to the call, when it was ascertained that the city would not only maintain them, but also their widows and children in case they fell in the service of their city; every rapscallion now had a wife, and became *père de famille*, and took care to enrol himself as such.

The most ridiculous scenes were enacted to keep up the excitement and frenzy of the people; some wretch would be dressed up as a miserable Croatian soldier, and taken out at one of the gates of the city, only to be made prisoner in the glacis, and brought in at another gate, and paraded through the streets, to show the valiant rabble what pitiful wretches their opponents were. Men who had died in the hospital were placed in coffins and paraded through the streets at the head of a company of armed ragamuffins as a respectable citizen, who had been entrapped by the military, mutilated and put to death outside the city walls. But the general military aspect of the city took a more regular form, from the time it was known that General Bem was in it. Patrols and guards were regularly posted and relieved, and outposts stationed beyond the exterior ramparts, on the lines, towards which the military were stationed; the bastions were more particularly looked to, and cannon placed so as to be used with effect, if necessary. But the general soon declared his opinion to the diet, that

Vienna could not be defended against a regular army; and although it might be put into a state of defence, to make a show of resistance, it was utterly useless to stand out unless the most efficacious assistance could be relied on from without.

The Emperor now issued another proclamation, stating that the continuance of the anarchical state of Vienna had placed him under the necessity of quelling the insurrection by force of arms—that public order was violated, and that the measures then about to be taken for restoring order would prevent the diet from continuing its deliberations within the city. He therefore declared that the diet should not assemble any longer in Vienna, and it was convoked to meet at Kremsier, on the 15th of November ensuing, where it might assemble, and continue its deliberations on the work of the constitution.

And now Prince Windishgrätz published his manifesto, and declared that within forty-eight hours the city must capitulate and lay down its arms, and that the armed body of work-people and students must be dissolved—that the university be closed, and twelve of the students sent to him as hostages—that other persons to be designated later should be delivered up to him—that all clubs be suppressed, and that martial law would be applied to all who should make the least resistance, or be taken with arms in their possession.

On the appearance of this proclamation the people became frantically alarmed, and left the city by thousands. Officers of the national guard abandoned their comrades and the service, and hid themselves in houses, cellars, and even the common sewers; women were every where endeavouring to conceal their most valuable effects, and confusion was at its height. Every male inhabitant was called on to assist in the fortification and defence of the city. The infatuated diet protested against the manifesto of the Prince as being illegal and hostile, as well to the rights of the people as to the throne—it also protested against the last proclamation of the Emperor, but at the same time it entered into a correspondence with the Prince to obtain favourable terms of surrender; but the Prince stood firm in his demands.

Messenhauser caused to be affixed to the walls orders, proclamations, and reports, as to the state of the army, couched in the most bombastic and absurd language, and breathing defiance to the summons to surrender, and calling on the people to die in the defence of their liberties!

The bewildered inhabitants at length became aware that the government had at last awakened to its responsibilities, and was acting in earnest; they found that bullying would not answer any longer, and, like arrant cowards, they fell at once into the deepest despair. The Hungarian army again crossed the Austrian frontiers, and Messenhauser, in order to reassure the drooping spirits of the people, took this opportunity to declare that a terrific battle would soon take place under the walls of Vienna, and that the diet had commanded him to establish a camp in the position of the Belvidere, and that he had begun to accomplish the duty, and that General Bem had been appointed its commander.

The diplomatic corps now thought it prudent to quit the city, which they did on the 23rd of the month, and on the same day the passage of the Imperial troops, concentrated from Bohemia and Moravia, took place over the Danube, by means of a bridge of boats, and the Prince established his camp at Hetzendorf; indeed the military, for some days past, to the number of seventy thousand men, had been gradually surrounding the whole city, and had already driven in the outposts of the insurgents, from the side of the Prater and Jagerzeil, and the city began to suffer from want of provision. A mobile corps was formed in haste, drawn from the very dregs of the people—they were commanded by some of the most desperate of the students, and if personal appearance could cause dismay to their enemies, surely they were enough to frighten the very devil; one would have supposed that they had dressed themselves up for the occasion—poo wretches! they were not so much to be blamed, and they were paid for what they did, and they only obeyed orders from their superiors, who had been bribed to do the like. In one of the chosen corps of this body, Robert Blum (who had arrived from Frankfort, and who was one of the deputies of the diet assembled in that city) volunteered to aid in the insurrection, and he was appointed captain of it by Messenhauser.

As the military took up their several positions at some distance round the exterior walls of the city, partial conflicts took place, and several sorties were ordered by General Bem, but no impression was made on the Imperial troops; the *prolétaires* complained loudly, however, that they were exposed to the enemy's fire, while the national guard were kept within the walls of the city.

The forty-eight hours granted by Prince Windishgrätz for the capitulation had now elapsed, but no preparations were made by the Viennese to surrender; constant firing of musketry continued during the night, and the troops drew in closer and closer, occupying or burning all the houses and buildings in their way.

Although the time allowed by the Prince had expired, he yet allowed twenty-four hours further before he ordered a general attack. This merciful delay had no beneficial result, and the morning of the 28th arrived, which was the most horrible and decisive day of the whole drama, for it was on this day that the republican flags, hitherto waving in the Praterstrasse, fell covered with dust and blood.

In the order of the day, Messenhauser had said, "Comrades! citizens! this day is decisive of our fate! Last evening a dispatch of the Ban Jellacic, addressed to his lieutenant commanding the troops in the Prater, was intercepted, by which we know the intentions and designs of the enemy." The Committee of Public Safety had ordered that, in case of any street-fighting, all the doors and windows should be kept open under pain of instant death, but an order had been previously made by Prince Windishgrätz, declaring that all doors and windows should be most scrupulously closed under pain of martial law—the wretched inhabitants had therefore to choose between the two.

The inner city of Vienna is so small that it may be traversed in any direction in half an hour—indeed it takes but three-quarters of an hour to walk the whole way round the bastions—beyond these bastions there is a fosse or ditch. All round the city, in a larger circle, is the glacis, which is planted with trees and laid out in walks ; there is an exception, however, to the suburb called the Leopoldstadt, which leads directly to the Prater, or Hyde Park of Vienna, and has no glacis.

At the extreme outer circle of the glacis commence the suburbs, of which there are thirty-four, and which surround the whole expanse, and these spread out in different directions like the rays of the sun ; there is an exterior wall around these suburbs, (with the exception of that part called the Prater, through which the Danube winds,) and which wall binds the whole city together ; beyond this exterior wall lie suburban villages and the open country, so that a bird's-eye view of Vienna may be likened (excepting towards the Prater) to a huge spider's web—the inner city being the insect itself lodged in the midst.

Messenhauser had transferred his quarters of observation on the morning of the 28th to the bastion of the inner city, named the Rothen Thurm Bastei; quite early a bombardment commenced against the lines beyond the exterior of the city. Very soon, however, a message came to Messenhauser, that the guards were in want of ammunition, and they demanded reinforcements. How was he to reply? he had neither the one nor the other at command. He answered drily, that he could not assist them; and, if they desired ammunition, they had better use their bayonets at once.

By nine in the morning, the general hospital for the sick, in the suburb Alservorstadt, and which contained about two thousand patients, was exposed to a sharp cannonade from the Imperial troops. To preserve this edifice, a drummer was sent in all haste to some distance from it, and there commanded to beat an alarm as loudly as possible—this was done, and it was soon perceived that the artillery of the Imperialists took another direction, and the hospital and sick were saved; the brave drummer continued to beat an alarm in the midst of a shower of balls, and Messenhauser rewarded him for his courage by a present of ten florins.

From the elevation of the tower of Saint Stephen's Cathedral, it was ascertained, that by ten o'clock all the lines were surrounded by a thick smoke from gunpowder, but through which the zigzag flash of the rockets and cannon shot was seen to make its lurid way. The most favourable point of attack was from the side of the north-east of the suburb called the Leopoldstadt, and the design of the assailants seemed to be to draw attention to other spots where they did not intend any serious attack. In the open parts of the Prater numerous battalions were now seen marching in battle array towards the Augarten; the most incessant cannonade was continued against the lines of Saint Marc and Mariahilf, two of the suburbs, although they were not for the present attacked by the infantry.

In the suburb of the Jägerzeil near the Prater, the vicar of the parish, moved by curiosity, mounted to the tower of his church, and peered through one of the windows; a few shot, however, soon satisfied his curiosity, and told him it was not child's play, and he was happy to retreat without being hurt; but the military kept so sharp a look out at the spires and towers of all the churches, that not an observation as to their movements could be taken.

An incessant firing was kept up against a huge stone barricade, called the Stern barricade, at the end of the Jägerzeil. The street was soon evacuated by all; but the windows of the houses on either side were occupied by students, national guards, and mobile guard, and balls were flying about in all directions. Another large barricade in this form

crossed the whole street of the Jägerzeil, a little higher up, and a flag with the three colours red, white, and yellow (being the Hungarian colours), and another of white, red, and green (the German union colours), were floating from it. At the corner of the street called the Sterngasse, behind that part of the barricade marked *a*, was posted General Bem. This barricade was defended by a battery of eighteen pounders: here the whistling of the grenades, the cannon balls, and musketry—the cries of the combatants—the falling of the roofs of the houses and of walls—the buildings in flames—the great number of dead and dying, and the groans of the wounded, formed a scene impossible fully to describe. The defenders of this barricade began to retire; but Bem encouraged them to remain, and threatened instant death to those who should attempt to retire. And now salvos of cannon from different parts burst on the ear; the fire from the batteries on the neighbouring hills against the suburbs became general, and the noise of the tocsin from the tower of Saint Stephen proclaimed in effect that the decisive hour was come; by eleven o'clock the cannonade in the Praterstrasse began to tell, and in half an hour the Stern barricade was taken possession of by the military: the Croatians stormed it most valliantly, and holding their swords between their teeth, with pistol in hand and others in their belt, they climbed up to the top and there fought their antagonists. The guard mobile fled, when they heard that the troops were already in the adjacent houses, and retired behind the second barricade, where were posted the eighteen pounders, commanded personally by Bem. The continued noise from the church bells in the suburbs as well as in the inner city, the drums beating the alarm, and aide-de-camps rushing furiously past, indicated the fact of a general battle along the lines. In the Jägerzeil, in the Rengasse, and at each end of all the streets of the suburb Leopoldstadt, there was furious and determined fighting; by twelve o'clock, nearly the whole of the outer portion of the suburb was in flames. And now might be seen an artillery officer gallopping to a spot where about a hundred men were posted to defend a building, and calling out "Retire—all is lost! the Croats are upon us!" Instant preparation was made to retire behind the first barricade in the Landstrasse, and horses harnessed to the cannon; but, whether by design or accident, they could not be made to move them.

The men retreated in haste, and the military coming up, took possession, not only of the cannon, but of all the ground up to the parish church of the Landstrasse. The assaulting columns put themselves in motion against the lines of Erdberg and Saint Marc; they found serious resistance at the gates, which were strongly barricaded, but they succeeded in gaining an entry into the suburb; and now, the incessant fire of musketry in volleys announced the commencement of barricade fighting throughout the suburbs. They were not, however, desperately defended, for after a few rounds of musketry the *prolétaires* retired behind others; but the greatest havoc was caused to the military by parties firing on them from the windows of the houses on either side, so that the troops were obliged to take the houses by storm, and hunt out or massacre all the inmates; the result of this was dreadful, for shortly were to be seen many of the students and *prolétaires* jumping, or being pitched out from the windows to the street; they were either shot dead before they fell, or received on the points of bayonets, and thus despatched.

The combat still continued in the Praterstrasse, where the most energetic resistance to the advance of the Imperial troops was still offered. And now the efforts of the military were redoubled; the greater part of the suburb Landstrasse was in their possession, and they continued to fight their way along the Praterstrasse; they had possession of the first barricade in the Jägerzeil, and now pointed cannon from the loopholes made for that purpose by the defenders, and commenced an awful cannonade against the second barricade, behind which continued the brave insurgent commander Bem; the five cannon at his disposal answered with great effect, and he was still enabled to hold out: there were at least three hundred of the *prolétaires*, with national guards, students, and strangers, at work here. While the combat continued, thus furiously at these points, the fate of the suburb Landstrasse was decided—the military had at length got possession of the whole, and the nature of the defence may be imagined by the fact that eighty bodies of the *prolétaires* were seen lying dead near the barricades. The suburb Leopoldstadt, where Bem was, still held out until five o'clock, and here the most blood was spilt. After having braved the concentrated energies of the military for two hours more, the barricade was at length turned on the side of the street Czerningasse, and attacked in the rear by the Imperial troops; a party of soldiers had penetrated into the houses laterally situated, and thence kept up a murderous fire on the defenders; they, however, in their turn were subject to the musketry of the *prolétaires* in the houses opposite; but this sort of combat could not now last long—the barricade and houses were obliged to be abandoned, and the troops rushed in victoriously. Towards evening a large number of the national guard threw away their arms (for more than a thousand muskets were found lying in the streets in the suburb Liechtenstall), but a number of women seized many of them, and cried out, "Shame on you, cowards! we will take your places!" and they actually divided themselves into companies—chose their chiefs from among the students—did military duty, and occupied some of the deserted posts. After the loss of the great barricade at the Jägerzeil, the whole suburb of the Leopoldstadt was abandoned by the insurgents, who retired within the inner city; after five o'clock in the day, the retreat became general, and hundreds of muskets were thrown into the canal.

The troops now approached the exterior ramparts all round the city, and on some points had penetrated and taken possession of parts of the suburbs, but the barricades were still obstinately defended, for the blood of the *prolétaires* was up, and they fought with the most determined energy and courage; the assailants contented themselves with the successes they had obtained. No serious attack had been made by the troops on the suburb Maria-hilf, but the batteries posted on the neighbouring heights had continued a devastating fire against it for many hours during the day, and caused much slaughter and burnings.

In the evening were to be seen fires in houses, buildings, and streets blazing on twenty-six different points of the suburbs and city: but the most violent was that in the Praterstrasse; there the whole length of the street was in flames.

The assault on the court-yard of the southern railroad, not far from the Belvedere gardens, was perhaps the most sanguinary and fatal to the cause of the insurgents—the defenders, composed for the most part of students and *prolétaires*, were surrounded by the troops, who thus cut off their retreat—they would not surrender, so that a few were made prisoners, and the remainder massacred.

General Bem had resided in the Jägerzeil until the 28th, and his carriage remained in the Stern gasse during the whole of the attack of that day; he was seated in a chair behind the great barricade during the fray. At about five o'clock, perceiving that it could no longer be defended, he entered his carriage and drove through the neighbourhood, giving various directions; in returning for the last time to the barricade, a ball whistled past quite close to him. When the barricade was taken by assault, he mounted a horse and rode to a neighbouring coffeehouse; he was slightly wounded by a spent musket ball: he then left this part of the suburb, and retired to the hotel of the minister of war in the Hof, and was conducted to an inn in the suburb Wieden: here he remained two days; and on the 30th, having procured for himself and two of his friends uniforms of Austrian officers, they dressed themselves as such, and rode coolly through the Austrian lines and made their escape to Hungary.

In the evening the chiefs of the insurrection assembled round Messenhauser, who now declared that all further defence of the city was useless, and proposed to enter into negociations with Prince Windishgrätz for the immediate surrender of the town: this was agreed to by all present and a deputation sent at once; the Prince remained firm to his own terms: but, he accorded them an armistice until midnight.

Early on the morning of the 29th Prince Windishgrätz was on the heights of Laerberg, on the look-out for the anticipated advance of the Magyars, and made his dispositions to receive them, but the whole day passed quietly ; towards evening, however, the Magyars appeared between Schwadorf and Schwechat, where they posted themselves on the heights. The Prince had expected a small part only of the Magyar force, and that the left wing of it would most probably appear at Himberg ; but he soon ascertained that they had advanced in great force, composed of all kinds of troops, and taken the road towards Wiener Neustadt. He immediately determined to attack them.

Messenhauser had early this morning called a peremptory meeting of the chiefs of the national guard, academic corps, and mobile guard ; he desired their public answer, yes or no, whether resistance should be continued? the universal answer was, "No;" and the act of capitulation was at once drawn up, and sent by a deputation to the Prince.

The news of the surrender of the city, without having demanded an amnesty for the revolted soldiers, caused the greatest consternation among them, and to the democrats who had seduced them from their duty. Armed men sought Messenhauser to put him to death; by eleven at night the fermentation was at its height—no order—no command: he who that night was eye-witness to the excesses committed—the fury—the hate—the despair of the revolted soldiers, and had examined their cadaverous countenances—declared that it was the most horrible of his life.

The deputation sent with the act of capitulation was received by the Prince with these words:

"I have waited for you so long that I scarcely thought to have seen you and had made my dispositions for the morrow, but as you are here, I will change them in your favour — your city shall receive no hurt." The act was then deposited in the hands of the Prince, and the deputation desired that the troops might be ordered to take possession of the city immediately.

"That cannot be," answered the Prince, "until the conditions I have already pointed out shall have been fulfilled; and, above all, that a general disarming shall take place, and the persons designated in a list in my hands delivered up to me — the persons in this list are Bem, Pulsky, Schütte, Messenhauser, Hauk, Braun, Fenneberg, Kuckenbecker, Burien, Hammerschmidt, Becker, Engländer, Tausenau, Gritzer, Deutsch and Mahler. These are the chiefs of the insurrection; and although I know that Schütte and Pulsky are no longer in Vienna, I look to you that the remainder do not escape; but to effectuate the disarming of the people, I shall expect another deputation from you to-morrow, who may be in a position to designate the places where all arms and cannon shall be transported; as soon as these are given up, I shall order my troops to enter the city." The deputation then returned to Vienna.

Early on the morning of the 30th, a troop of women, with drums beating, muskets at the shoulder, Calabrian hats and red caps on the head, and pistol in belt, passed through the streets, shouting that the Hungarians had arrived; this measure strongly excited the mobile guard and *prolétaires*, who again flew to their arms; the second deputation to Prince Windishgrätz had proceeded to. his quarters, and having accomplished their duties, were returning to the city with the details of the capitulation, and which were to be put in execution immediately. But even while these parties were treating on the conditions with the prince, conflicts again took place in some of the suburbs; the revolutionary party would not acknowledge the capitulation, and tore down the placards announcing the details of the act, and insisted that the Magyars were on the way to their assistance. In fact, from the tower of Saint Stephen a dense mass of smoke was observable near Schwechat, and reports of cannon were distinctly heard in that direction; but the intense fog hindered any telescopic observation. All Vienna rushed to the roofs of the houses, to ascertain the facts. Messenhauser and his council, the President of the diet, and many members, the President of the committee of students, the commander of the mobile corps and of the academic legion, all met together, and waited the coming events in the greatest excitement.

From eleven to two the noise of the battle seemed to approach the city walls, but the fog continuing, nothing certain could be ascertained; the direction the battle took could only be guessed at by flashes from the cannon.

The anxious multitude covered Messenhauser with reproaches for having advised the capitulation, and called on him to report to them and the people the exact progress of the battle. He was now on the tower of the cathedral, and was strongly embarrassed—he feared to declare openly that the capitulation had taken place, or to say what he knew respecting the battle; but being menaced by some of the democrats, he turned to a member of the diet near him, to know how he should act; this man nodding his head, Messenhauser hesitated no longer, and wrote down the first, and afterwards the second, and other bulletins, which informed the people of the progress of the battle. The first bulletin was as follows:—

"From the tower of Saint Stephen it can be distinctly seen that a battle is taking place near Kaiser Ebersdorf, but neither the troops nor the progress of the fight can be distinguished."

The effect of this news to the mob was magical; a vast crowd of the lower orders of both sexes had filled the body of the cathedral; reports that the Hungarians were gaining the day were spread among them, and they all rushed to their arms, crying out—

"To arms! to arms! to the assistance of the Hungarians!"

All seemed electrified by the news, and the revolutionary party again succeeded in fanaticising the city.

The second bulletin now appeared; it stated—"That the battle seemed to take the direction of Oberlaa and Inzersdorf, but the fog hindered it from being closely observed. It seemed as if the Hungarians were advancing victoriously, and declared that in the event of a beaten army approaching the city walls, it was the duty of all armed citizens to hold themselves in readiness."

The third bulletin speedily followed—the announcement was, that a large body of troops was in the distance, but it could not be distinguished whether they were of cavalry or of infantry. On the left of Schwechat, between Kaiser Ebersdorf and Mannswörth, the combat was concentrated. From the incessant flashes of the cannon the number of the batteries could be counted. During the last hour the battle had evidently been approaching nearer and nearer to the walls of Vienna.

An order was now forwarded by Messenhauser to the chief of the national guards of the suburb Wieden, to the effect that, if the two armies should fight before the walls of Vienna, it was the duty of each national guard to place himself under arms; the whole body was therefore to assemble immediately, to contribute to defend their hearths. All the posts round the city were to be re-occupied, and they were to keep themselves in readiness to succour all points menaced, and to endeavour to maintain order within the city walls.

In consequence of these bulletins, the armed masses, excited by the chief of the insurrection, could no longer be held in, and they occupied the bastions and all the positions as before the capitulation. Many persons now forced themselves upon Messenhauser, to extract an order from him to attack the military, but by this time he was well aware of the result of the battle between the Austrians and Magyars; he answered—

"No, all resistance is useless, the means of further defence are exhausted—we have no longer any hope of success; for, with my own eyes, I have seen that the Hungarians are completely beaten."

The whole night was passed in riot and intoxication; the insurgents knew that they had broken the terms of the capitulation, and expected no mercy, and the miserable inhabitants looked forward to the city being taken by storm and sacked by the military in the morning.

Prince Windishgrätz having been informed of all that had passed in the city, saw himself obliged to take possession by force, and he ordered the bombardment to take place the next day.

On the 31st of October, at three o'clock, the principal attack of the troops took place against that part of the city called the Burg (palace). The troops, after having taken the suburbs by storm, advanced to the glacis; and now a tremendous cannonade was opened against the city; the population was seized with the utmost fear; grenades, bombs, shells, congreve rockets, and shot of six and twelve pounds flew through the city like hail, houses fell, conflagrations broke out, and most of the inhabitants rushed for shelter to the cellars or caves under ground; the noise of the cannonade was augmented by the crash of the fall of walls and stacks of chimneys; the streets were completely empty, but here and there were seen piles of arms, military clothing and decorations thrown from the various windows, so that some of the principal streets looked as if they were depositories of military stores. One man, at the first floor of a corner house in the Karnthnerstrasse, was watching the motion of the balls in the air, with his arms folded on the sill of the window, when a ball dropped and crushed them both! Four balls entered the roof of the hotel Archduke Charles, and would have caused a conflagration had they not been instantly cooled by water; many of the houses in this street were kept from burning only by the constant application of water by their occupants. The residences of the diplomatic corps suffered much; cannon balls and shells entered the windows of the Prussian embassy—the French embassy received many balls—the English embassy lost a huge stack of chimneys—the Turkish embassy had been previously riddled with shot, for that was situated in the Leopoldstadt, and it would have been entirely destroyed had not the *maître-d'hotel* dressed himself in haste in his master's clothes, and rushing into the street, declared to the assaulting Croatians that he was the ambassador, and that his house was therefore sacred! The houses near the Kärnthner gate were dreadfully cut about by the cannonade. On one of the houses, (and there were ten or twelve in the row between the gate and the palace of Count Kolorat similarly punished,) sixty-three indentations from cannon balls were counted—the wood-work was burnt and crushed, the roof on fire, and the stone and cement (of which the houses were built) crumbled and broken away: the palace of Count Kolorat, at the corner, was a complete prey to the flames. The Imperial library, forming part of the palace, was burning, and the roof and tower of the church of Saint Augustine were completely destroyed.

One of the communal guards hung out from the walls near the Burgthor, a white flag, which caused a cessation of firing from the military ; they advanced to enter the gate, but volleys of musketry and cannon-shot proved the treachery of the act, and exasperated the troops beyond measure. This act of perfidy was the last committed ; for the troops, having now burst open the gate by cannon, rushed in and took possession of the whole ground up to the doors of the palace, which were now similarly cannonaded and stormed. A little later the troops effected an entrance at the Kärnthner gate, took possession of that part of the city, and the Leopoldstadt and Landstrasse pouring in their contingents, the whole city was in vested and occupied; the troops aided in extinguishing the fires amid the acclamations of the people, who received them as liberators from the hateful tyranny under which they had been kept by the democrats for so long a period. The military occupied all the public squares, and bivouaced in the streets by thousands, and cannon was posted at every opening. Thus was the combat concluded, and the city taken; the loss of the insurgents was computed at two thousand men, and the military could scarcely have sustained an inferior loss.

CHAPTER IV.

It is in the nature of the thing, that, on the settlement of a truce, owing to the hurry with which the general terms are stated, many incidents remain unforeseen and unsettled ; and that immediately after its commencement, difficult points present themselves, from which each of the contracting parties may deduce a right for the suspension or evasion of the treaty, as soon as it may appear convenient. Thus it was with the truce of Milan. The terms of the convention were: 1st, that the line of demarcation was to be that of the frontiers of each country; 2nd, that the fortresses of Peschiera, Rocca d'Aufo and Osopo, should be delivered up by the Sardinian troops to the Austrians; 3rd, that Modena and Parma, as well as the city of Piacenza, with the territory of the fortress, should be evacuated by the Sardinian troops; 4th, that the Sardinian troops, as well on land as at sea, should evacuate Venice and the Venetian territory; 5th, that, in all the places abovementioned, property should be respected by the Austrians; 6th, that the armistice should endure for six weeks, and, that after the expiration of this time, it should either be prolonged, or hostilities re-commence after the armistice should have been denounced eight days previously.

One of the most difficult points was, the evacuation of those fortresses, the commanders of which did not belong to the Sardinian army; and they, therefore, thought it right not to acknowledge the acts of the king. Then, again, upon the first news of the surrender of Milan, the city of Venice had solemnly recalled her resolution of the 4th of July, acknowledging Charles Albert as chief of Upper Italy, and incorporating Venice with the kingdom of Sardinia, and had again constituted herself a republic. From the 15th to the 23rd of July, three Piedmontese reserve battalions had entered that city in the name of the king; and, on the 6th of August, royal commissioners from Charles Albert had assumed the chief authority; but as early as the 10th, the republic of Saint Marc was proclaimed. On this day the people rose in masses, and attempted to seize the commissioners, who, however, were enabled to escape on board ship; but the Piedmontese flag was pulled down, and that of the Venetians hoisted in its stead. Manin appeared most opportunely, and was hailed as dictator. Though the evacuation of Venice was not declared in the convention, with the same precision as the surrender of the fortresses of the Italian continent, yet Radetzky appeared to have expected the surrender of all those forts, which the Piedmontese, either by themselves or their party, really occupied; amongst which Venice was to be included; but when it was called on to surrender, it flatly refused, relying on its impregnable situation. In fact, it is seated at the northern division of a lake of sea water, about thirty miles long and six broad. It is protected from the violence of the Adriatic by three tongues of land from north to south. Ships of small tonnage can pass up through these tongues of land, which are strongly defended by forts on both banks; the south entrance is protected by another fort called the Brondolo, which, although near twenty miles from the city, is considered a most important position and is fortified accordingly; an immense fort had also been erected at the western part of the lake, about four miles distant from the city, and this was the famous fort Malghera.

The Piedmontese, instead of answering the summons to surrender, by giving up possession according to the spirit of the treaty, relinquished the forts to volunteers, ten thousand of whom, from all parts of Italy, had arrived, and thought of further maintaining themselves in this city. The generals delayed the embarkation of the Piedmontese troops, to put this plan into execution; and this flagrant act induced Radetzky to detain a Piedmontese artillery park of eighty large guns, which was, according to the treaty, to have left Peschiera. This last-named fortress had been invested since the 26th of July, on the town side, but the garrison was, nevertheless, supplied with provisions by the steamers of the lake.

On the evening of the 9th of August, the bombardment of it began from thirty-two pieces of ordnance, and was continued throughout the 10th, up to the time of the arrival of the news of the truce; when, after some delay, the fortress was delivered up to the Austrians. Rocca d'Aufo was also surrendered, but the commandant of Osopo, on the contrary, refused to attend to the summons to surrender, and held out until October, when, indeed, he gave up possession, on honourable conditions, to a battalion of Austrian troops, which had stood before it for five months and a half.

By Radetzky's bold advance upon Milan, the retreat was cut off, by the Ticino, to all the detached divisions of troops of the Piedmontese left wing. The truce, however, secured them a free marching off through the Austrian armies to their own country; and General Durando, who had retired with three thousand men to Bergamo, hastened to profit by this permission; but other Lombard commanders, on the contrary, thought it for the interest of Italian unity, to disapprove the truce, and called the king's deportment and acts by the name of treason; they determined to continue the war on their own account, and, in case of non-success, they thought that they could retreat into neutral Switzerland.

Garibaldi, with four thousand men, went over Lugano to the Piedmontese shore, and to the upper part of Lago Maggiore. Griffini, who had tarried too long in Brescia, retreated at the approach of General D'Aspre, with two thousand five hundred men and twenty cannon, over Edolo to Tirano, and threw himself into the Swiss valley of Poschiavo; thither also proceeded the volunteers commanded by D'Aspice coming from Tonale. Besides these considerable divisions, many single Piedmontese soldiers, cut off from their corps, entered the Swiss territory, and many from the civil service also hurried to that country. The appearance of these fugitives offered the truest image of the history of the war. In ragged clothes, whose originally dark blue colour had been changed into a blackish grey tint, the brave Piedmontese soldier hurried by the shortest cut to his country. More slowly went those crusaders, among whom were some tall powerful men, with tremendous long beards, whose well preserved blouses, decorated by the red cross, did not betray great exertions in the field of war; and still less soldier-like was the appearance of the young gentry from the large towns, who, still dressed in elegant chasseur and sharpshooter regimentals, sported their figures in the public walks.

In Switzerland, committees were formed to satisfy the wants of the needy strangers. It is notorious that the Italian is ordinarily close and needy; but most of the fugitives, being merchants, lawyers, medical men, and authors, now cheerfully gave their utmost to support their poorer countrymen.

The dukedom of Modena was taken possession of by Prince Liechtenstein, in the name of its lawful sovereign ; and that of Parma was occupied by General Thurn, for the like purpose. General Weldon had, however, passed the papal frontiers, and stood before Bologna (to which city some Austrian officers, relying on the treaty, had betaken themselves, but when there, they were brutally murdered), and made preparations for a bombardment, and actually proceeded to this extremity when he received superior orders to retire. The evacuation of the ecclesiastical states was soon accomplished ; and a treaty, concluded at Ferrara, provisionally settled most points in dispute, between the two countries. The territory of Tuscany was not occupied by the Austrians, as the

Grand Duke had declared that he was able and willing to maintain peace and order by himself.

Tranquillity appeared now to be re-established in all Upper Italy, when, contrary to the will of the Piedmontese authorities, and the Helvetic confederacy, the Lombard party chief, Garibaldi, made an irruption into Lombardy, with a large band of armed refugees, in order to carry on a guerilla warfare, in the mountain districts round the Italian lakes. For some days he succeeded in roving about and levying contributions, and had obtained some advantages over small isolated Austrian detachments; but as soon as General D'Aspre was sent with a considerable force against him, this guerilla war ceased. The most considerable incident that occurred during this robber-like expedition was, at a combat which took place near Merazzone not far from Varese. Here Garibaldi, held the place with fifteen hundred men, and maintained it against the attack of the Austrians till late at night, but reinforcements having arrived to the Imperialists, Garibaldi prudently withdrew, favoured by darkness, and arrived at Lucino, where he was lost sight of, and his adherents dispersed themselves.

The Austrians were not in a position to act offensively against the city of Venice until October. But their most energetic endeavours were made to obtain possession of the fort of Malghera. It is a low fortress, built on the level of the water with ramparts of earth, and no stone walls, having six lunettes to the land side, with one hundred pieces of cannon pointed in all directions, and capable of containing about four thousand five hundred men; it is only accessible by the slip of land leading to Mestre, and it is surrounded on all sides by deep marshes, and the waters of the salt lake. Trenches were opened by the

Austrians on the Mestre road; but the inhabitants of Venice having cut one of the canals in the vicinity, the whole ground occupied by the Austrians was inundated. From Mestre, however, an incessant firing was kept up from the batteries, and replied to by the fort of Malghera; but still nothing effectual was accomplished, and this cross firing was kept up languidly during the winter.

Immediately on the occupation of Vienna by the Imperial troops, Prince Windishgrätz issued a manifesto declaring the city and surrounding country in a state of siege; that the academic legion was dissolved, as also the national guard (which, however, it was contemplated, might be re-organised at a later period); that a general disarming must take place; that all political associations and clubs should be suppressed; that not more than five persons should assemble together in any public place; and the application of martial law to the originators and assistants of the revolt; and he nominated Baron Corden as commander of the city. A few days later, General Weldon was nominated governor of Vienna, and charged with the direction of all measures necessitated by the state of siege.

The first man who suffered under martial law, was Robert Blum, who had left his own country to join the revolutionary party at Vienna. The next was Messenhauser, the late commandant of the city, and whose life would probably have been spared, had it not been for his participation in the acts of the democrats on the 30th of October. They were both shot, according to sentence of court martial.

The Emperor now issued a manifesto to the people of Hungary, Croatia, Transylvania, Sclavonia, and the military frontiers, notifying that Prince Windishgrätz had been charged with the mission of re-establishing order and peace in Hungary, and the King therefore, expected that the laws would be obeyed; he condemned all illegal attempts against private property, and forbade the emission of paper money, as well as any levy of troops or of the people. He declared that all the acts and decisions of the late Hungarian diet were of no effect; and that Louis Kossuth and his partizans were traitors to the throne and country.

It was clear, that, by the invasion of the Austrian soil, near Schwechat, by the Magyars, the question of open war against Hungary had become decided. That country could only be preserved to the monarchy by force of arms; and it was necessary that it should be conquered, to nullify the germs of dismemberment, which had now, for so long been fostered everywhere.

Prince Windishgrätz had been clothed with the most extensive powers, and he summoned all generals, officers, and soldiers, who had swayed from their duty to return, and accorded until the 26th of November for that purpose. After that day, those who should not respond to the call were to be considered traitors to their country, and dealt with accordingly. By the middle of November, the principal part of the army was concentrated on the plains of Vienna, ready to penetrate into Hungary. But as yet the commissariat was in a very defective state, and the strength of the insurgents and the position of their army were not known.

Before the principal part of the Imperial army was ordered to cross the frontier, the marshal had commanded that the different corps, destined to act separately, should accelerate their movements, so as to combine their operations with the principal army. He had ordered them to advance from their several points of starting in a direct line to Buda-Pesth. His plan was to operate a general concentration of his whole army at the capital of Hungary; and, however simple this idea was, it required some time to put it into execution.

At the same time that Prince Windishgrätz was completing his preparations for the invasion of Hungary, the diet had assembled at Kremsier, in pursuance of the mandate of the Emperor; and Prince Schwarzenberg, who had been chosen prime minister, detailed at the first sitting the intentions of ministers in their future administration of the country. With much firmness and energy he declared to the diet, that he was charged with the executive, and that he accepted the vast responsibility, firmly resolved to set aside all unconstitutional influence, but, at the same time, to repress all endeavours to lessen the executive power: he declared that he desired a constitutional monarchy, —sincerely and without guile—that the Lombardo-Venetian kingdom, organically united to the Austrian constitutional monarchy, should find the most certain guarantees for its nationality; that the violation of these sacred rights had lighted up civil war in Hungary, but that peace should be restored by force of arms; and that the great task to be accomplished by him, was to find a new lien, which should attach and reunite all the nationalities of the monarchy, so as to form one great state.

And now an act of high historical importance took place, which unshakled the hands of ministers in their policy towards Hungary, namely the abdication of the Emperor Ferdinand. It was well known that the promises and concessions he had made to the Hungarians had fettered the whole policy of ministers in this respect; and the oaths he had taken, at the time of his coronation, militated strongly against the measures now absolutely necessary to be adopted, for the extinction of the rebellion. His successor was not bound by the oaths of his predecessor, and could therefore act without the scruples attributed to him.

On the 2nd of December, therefore, the Emperor and Empress, surrounded by the Imperial family, went to the great room of the archiepiscopal palace at Olmutz, where were assembled Prince Windishgrätz, the Ban of Croatia, Jellacic, Prince Schwarzenberg,and all the ministers. Here the monarch declared, after reading the act of abdication, that he abandoned his rights to his legitimate successor, the Archduke François Charles. After this, the Archduke François Charles read the document of his resignation to the succession in favour of his eldest son; and then the declaration of the majority of the young Emperor François Joseph was announced. At this moment, the young Emperor threw himself on his knees before his father, and demanded his blessing. The

Emperor Ferdinand, during this act, had advanced towards Prince Windishgrätz and Baron Jellacic, and, taking them by the hand, led them to his successor, and they rendered their homage, visibly affected. The doors of the palace were then thrown open, and the acts of abdication and of resignation were made public. The late Emperor and Empress immediately afterwards quitted Olmutz, to take up their future residence at Prague.

The new Emperor François Joseph immediately issued a manifesto, which, after noticing the abdication of his uncle, and the renunciation of the crown by his father in his favour, stated, that in virtue of his natural and legal rights, and in pursuance of the stipulations of the Pragmatic Sanction, he had taken possession of the government of all his states, including the kingdom of Hungary, and the principality of Transylvania. That at the moment, when, if he could follow the dictates of his heart, it would have afforded him the greatest happiness to forward the prosperity of his Hungarian subjects, the accomplishment of his intentions had become impossible. That the manœuvres of a criminal faction had assured him that, as that portion of his Hungarian subjects remaining faithful to the reigning dynasty could not prove their fidelity and attachment by overt acts, it was his duty to deliver them from the tyranny and oppression under which they suffered. That, in consequence, the Emperor sanctioned all the resolutions which had been taken by his predecessor, on the 6th and 7th of November preceding; and subjected all public authorities to the strictest responsibility in their execution of them. He confirmed the nomination of Prince Windishgrätz, as Commander-in-chief of the army, with unlimited powers to re-establish order and peace, and he commanded his misguided troops in Hungary and Transylvania, to submit themselves to his orders. He trusted, with full confidence, in the good sense and innate fidelity of his peaceful subjects in Hungary and Transylvania, that they would rigorously resist all criminal seductions of the rebels, and that they would endeavour, in their circle, to support the intentions of the Emperor for their good; and he hoped that they would assist in hastening on the moment, most ardently wished for by him, when it would be permitted him, under the protection of God, to address to them words of peace, unity, and confidence.

These occurrences caused a short delay in the operations of the Austrian army, but which delay was a great gain to the Magyars; such a gain, indeed, that it proved the lever of the insurrection. General Georgey, who had been appointed Commander-in-chief of the army of the insurgents, by Kossuth, in the stead of Moga, had issued a manifesto, in which he declared that the committee of defence (of which Kossuth was the soul) was the organ of the representatives of the people for the legal government of the country, and that it declared the will of the majority of the nation, and ought to be obeyed.

As soon as the acts relating to the abdication of the Emperor Ferdinand, and the succession of his nephew, François Joseph, came to the knowledge of the diet at Pesth, that body came to a resolution, and formally declared, that, without the consent of the nation at large, the royal throne of Hungary, according to law and all custom, could not become vacant but by the decease of the king; that, if such a death should occur, then the successor to the throne was obliged to swear obedience to the laws of the kingdom, and to the safeguard of the constitution; and to cause himself to be crowned with the diadem of St. Stephen; that, in the present circumstances, therefore, the abdication of the throne by the Emperor Ferdinand was invalid without the assent of the people; that he had no right to abdicate in favour of his brother or his nephew, when he still might have children of his own, who would be his legitimate successors; and that, if the actual sovereign felt himself unable to bear the weight of the crown of Hungary, a regency, or provisional government, should have been appointed and formed to carry on the kingly power; so that, as the spontaneous abdication of the Emperor in no wise changed the constitution, nor the organic laws of the country, the diet, as the recognized legal organ of the people, declared that no one could dispose of the Hungarian crown without its consent, and that they who did not adopt this opinion should be regarded as traitors to their country.

On this Kossuth framed a new oath for the army; and he immediately influenced the clergy to preach a crusade against the Imperialists as the enemies of his country; and the better to induce the people to flock to his standard, he declared that all persons who should lose a limb in actual service, or be invalided from wounds received, should, at their own choice, either receive from the country ten acres of land in perpetuity, or one thousand florins in good money.

He also appointed ministers to the different departments of the government, keeping finance for himself; giving Messaros that of war; Casimir Batthyanyi, the exterior; Nyari, the interior; Madaras, police; Pulsky, commerce; and Szemere, justice; but none of these individuals took upon themselves the title.

By the 14th of December Prince Windishgrätz had completed his preparations, and he divided his army into three corps. The first was under the Ban Jellacic, the second under Count Wrbna, and the third under the Duke Serbiloni. He at once transferred his general quarters to Fishament, the Ban was at Haimbourg, and Count Wrbna at Schwechat. A strong brigade, resting its left wing on the Danube, occupied the whole frontier by Wolfsthal, Berg, and Edelsthal, as far as Petronell, where it joined itself to another, which extended itself by Sommerein the whole length of the Leitha, having its right wing covered by a detached corps under the command of Colonel Horwath; two brigades formed the advanced guard, on the left bank of the Danube, as far as Marcheck; a bridge of boats near Deutsch-Altenbourg kept up a communication between the two banks of the river.

On the 15th of December the Marshal transferred his quarters to Petronell, and the Ban proceeded to Bruck; and on that evening offensive operations against Hungary commenced.

Colonel Horwath, with about three thousand men, formed the extreme right flank. To cover his right wing, he sent two companies and two squadrons of light horse towards Oedenbourg; this column met a detachment of the Magyar army, forming the advanced guard of a body of twelve thousand men under General Perczel. This detachment had possession of a number of houses in a village, from whence they kept up a lively fire against the Austrians; but the village was soon taken, and the Hungarians retreated; the remainder of the corps proceeded towards Oedenbourg. On the heights of Krausdorf a detachment of Magyars was observed, which retired immediately; and the Austrians marched on to the town of Oedenbourg and occupied it, their enemy having previously retired.

The army of the Magyars, thirty thousand strong, occupied the whole line from the lake of Neusiedel to the right bank of the Danube, and it was under the command of the celebrated General Geörgey; he was the most intelligent and moderate in his political views, of all the insurgent chiefs.

Prince Windishgrätz advanced from Bruck to make a *reconnoissance*, and, after a few shots were exchanged between the advanced guards, the Hungarians retired. The Austrians were enabled to advance, for no serious opposition was presented to them, and by the 18th of December they took possession of Presburg, the insurgents having retired from that city, when the inhabitants sent a deputation to the Marshal, offering their submission. But long before the principal army of the Austrians had begun the offensive, General Simunich had crossed the Carpathian Mountains, and had entered the valley of the Waag; but the superior forces of the Magyars had forced him to retire as far as Golding. Having received considerable reinforcements, he was enabled soon to take the offensive again, and arrived near Tyrnau. Here the insurgents offered a determined resistance to his further progress; but, after two hours hard fighting, Simunich gained the day, and the insurgents retired.

Another detached corps of the Austrians had advanced by Jablunka, and, although it had penetrated as far as Sillein on the Waag, it was obliged to operate its retreat before the superior forces of the enemy; reinforcements were also sent here, and they were then enabled to advance to Trenschin. General Schlik was entrusted with the command of the third detached column, and he had made himself master of Eperies, but he there learnt that Mészáros, with near thirty thousand Hungarians, and thirty-two cannon, was prepared to attack him, and to force his retreat across the Carpathian mountains. Schlik boldly resolved to make an attack, and pushed on, in the night, to gain the position of Budimir; a brigade was sent in to the side of the river

Hernath, to turn the point of Budimir, and find a ford, and to menace Kaschau. Having attacked the insurgents, and forced them to retire, Schlik carried the heights of Budimir after a short but decisive combat. In the supposition that the brigade sent by the river side had arrived at the spot agreed on, he advanced to throw the enemy between himself and it, but he was deceived—no detachment had arrived, and Mészáros gained the road to Kaschau. Nothing daunted, however, Schlik resolved to gain possession of this town; the river was forded, and although the detachment experienced serious loss in this service, yet on the approach of the whole body, the city hoisted a white flag, and surrendered.

In the mean time the Ban Jellacic, had ordered a general *reconnoissance*, and although several skirmishes took place, the Magyars, under Geörgey, did not show any determined resistance, but retired to Raab. It was supposed here, from the preparations Geörgey had made, that a determined resistance would be offered to the Austrians, and the city stoutly defended; but it was soon seen that he merely wished to gain time, and effect his junction with the corps under Perczel. The disposition of the Austrian army, however, prevented his doing so, and he retreated with his whole forces towards Buda.

Prince Windishgrätz entered Raab, which city was illuminated on the occasion. He sent a brigade of cavalry in pursuit of his enemy, which came up with the rear, and took about seven hundred prisoners. During these movements, Colonel Horwath had attained to Kapuvar, thus flanking the right wing of the principal army. Another detachment arrived at Stein-am-Anger to open a communication with a body of nine thousand six hundred men, commanded by General Nugent, which was advancing from Styria by Loevoe.

Perczel, finding that Geörgey had retired from Raab, retreated also by Jánosháza to gain Stuhlweissenbourg, and rejoin the principal army of the Magyars near Buda. The Ban Jellacic, to disturb this plan, took the road to Stuhlweissenbourg, and having encountered Perczel at the head of about ten thousand men, attacked him with resolution and success. After some hard fighting, the result of which was the loss of sixteen cannon and one thousand prisoners on the part of Perczel, he retired with the remainder of his troops towards Stuhlweissenbourg.

The second corps of the Austrian army in its advance, now appeared before the fortress of Comorn, and summoned it to surrender, but its commandant, Maithenyi, flatly refused. As it was not part of the present plan of operations to lose any time before any isolated place, the Austrian corps proceeded on its march, leaving a detachment only to observe the fortress; the isle of Shuett was occupied by an Austrian division, and the north was protected by detachments from the corps of Simunich.

Schlik, Simunich, and Horwath still pressed forward toward Buda-Pesth—but they, as well as the principal army, were closely watched, and sometimes attacked by Mészáros, who had a great force in their neighbourhood. The insurgents, however, continued to retire, and keep out of sight and reach, and by the 3rd of January, 1849, they were perceived by the Austrians posted on the heights of Buda. In the afternoon of this day, a deputation from the Hungarian diet, at the head of whom, however, was Count Louis Batthyanyi, arrived at the general quarters of the Marshal to treat; but he refused to see them, and exacted an unconditional submission. It was now fully expected that there would be some serious fighting, as the third corps of the Austrian army was concentrated before

Buda, and in its neighbourhood; but the policy of the Magyars was not yet sufficiently advanced for them to risk a general battle, and they again retired, taking their way towards Debreczin. Kossuth and his party had, however, already published bulletins of victories obtained over the Austrians, whose sudden appearance under the walls of the capital astonished the Hungarians not a little.

The Prince entered Buda on the 5th of January without striking a blow, and the whole advance of the Austrian army had seemed almost like a triumphal march. It was now that the unfortunate Count Louis Batthyanyi was taken prisoner, he had a particular appointment at Pesth, and thought that he could keep it, and yet be in time to effect his escape, before the Austrians should take possession of the city, but he stayed one half hour too late; as he was passing the outskirts of the city in his carriage, he came up with a party of Austrians just previously posted in the immediate locality, who at once seized him and his retinue, and conveyed them to Pesth, where they were all safely lodged in captivity.

In possession of Buda, Prince Windishgrätz immediately made dispositions to occupy the strategic points of Waitzen and Szolnok, and proceeded to the pacification of the country thus far occupied by him. He divided it into three military districts; the first, containing the counties of Presburg, Neutra, Trentschin, Arwa, Liptau, Turocz, Sohl, Barsch and Comorn (although the fortress still remained in possession of the insurgents) was confided to General Kempen; the second formed by the counties of Pesth, Albe-Royale, Gran, and the districts of Cumanie and Jazig, to General Wrbna; and the third, composed of the counties of Baranya, Raab, and Wieselbourg to General Buricz; their duty was to pacify the country; to preside at all councils of war; to supervise the transport of food, and to provide for the hospitals; but they had not sufficient forces with them to attain these desirable objects, for although the country was occupied by the Austrians, the inhabitants were inimical to them.

The affairs of Transylvania also occupied the attention of Prince Windishgrätz. Kossuth had succeeded in raising the Szeklers; with their assistance, and numbers of Magyar partisans, the revolutionary faction, headed by the celebrated General Bem, here mustered its strength, and had terrorized the whole country. General Puchner, with his small force, was obliged to retire to the south of Transylvania, and there act only on the defensive. General Bem, whose activity and energy were proverbial, had in a short space of time collected an army of thirty thousand men completely armed and equipped, and provided with artillery, and all munitions of war.

Against such a force, no Austrian corps, stationed in that part of the country, could stand, and they speedily retired ; a brigade arriving from Gallicia, fortunately re-established a communication with the corps from the south, and it was resolved by the Austrians to make a general attempt against Clausenburg ; but instead of attacking, it was found that they themselves were attacked, and compelled again to retire.

The combined forces, however, under Generals Urban and Wardener, were enabled to effect the reduction of the city on the 17th of November, and on the 20th they were reinforced by a strong division under General Kaliani, but in the mean time the insurgent commanders Katona, Miklos, and Teleki Sandor, had occupied Deesch, and a strong concentration of them took place near Csucsa. The Austrians had resolved on an attack ; but at this moment an order arrived from

General Puchner, to detach a brigade towards the south against the Szeklers, even at the risk of evacuating Clausenberg. Urban (the general commanding) proposed to evacuate this town at once, and turn their entire force against the Szeklers; but this proposition was rejected at a council, and from this time began the defection and division of the Austrian forces, which became so disastrous, and from which the enemy derived so much advantage; attacking various places at once with small forces, they were beaten everywhere. Bem saw his advantage, and pursued it to the utmost, and it was almost by a miracle that the Austrian troops were saved; after a march of thirty hours without food or repose, the column arrived at Saint Joseph. Here Urban hoped to hold the district; but the enemy, having concentrated a considerable force, attacked him, and he was obliged to retire to Pajana-Stampi, in Bucovina. The Imperial troops had possession of the defile of Tihutza, but the energetic General Bem attacked this defile, carried it, and entering Bucovina, forced the Austrian outposts at Dorna to retire. Urban again retreated as far as Kimpolung and Jakobeny. Thus, in the short space of eight days, the whole of the north of Transylvania was in the hands of General Bem. This indefatigable soldier, having left a sufficient frontier garrison, marched his troops against General Puchner.

The Magyars had concentrated considerable forces in Southern Hungary, in the Banat, and in the neighbourhood of Temesvar. It was here, it will be recollected, that the civil war had commenced, and had acquired its greatest activity. General Rukawina had from the beginning guessed the revolutionary projects of Kossuth and the Hungarian ministry, and had opposed them to the utmost of his power, and he had been seconded by the Servians; nevertheless the fortresses of Peterwardein and

Esseg had declared in favour of the revolution, and had hoisted the Hungarian tricolor flag. The insurgents had assembled a force of forty thousand men in the Banat; and it was commanded by Casimir Batthyanyi, Vetter, and Mariassy; they had no concerted plan of operations, but fought, sometimes together, sometimes separately; their principal aim was to obtain possession of the fortresses of Arad and Temesvar, which continued to be garrisoned by troops faithful to the Austrians. These fortresses were invested, and reduced to a most deplorable condition, the garrison being obliged to live on horseflesh; but, at this epoch, an unexpected success having been obtained by Count Leinengen over the insurgents, the communication between these two fortresses was re-established, and six months' provisions and reinforcements introduced. This state of things had lasted till the end of December, but at this date Count Leinengen was obliged to retire to the neighbourhood of Temesvar, for General Rukawina being menaced by the superior forces of the enemy, was compelled to relinquish all thought of extensive operations, and to provide only for the protection of the fortress of Temesvar. On all other points the insurgents had shown equal activity—a corps was stationed between Titel and Pancsowa. Werschetz was occupied by nine thousand men, and they also held possession of Weisskirchen and Lagerndorf. The frontiers of Gallicia were not even safe from the incursions of the insurgents, and they were thence provided with all kinds of material to carry on the war, and with provisions to an unlimited extent.

The higher valleys of the Waag and of Arwa were also exposed, so long as General Simunich continued to besiege the small fortress of Leopoldstadt; and the tardiness of this operation paralyzed the efforts of the corps before Comorn, and in the island of Shüett. The insurgents profited by these delays, by sending large detachments, and making sorties either towards the north, and in the rear of the Austrians, and a sortie from the fortress of Comorn forced the blockading corps to retire as far as Wartberg. Such was the general situation of the country when Prince Windishgrätz took possession of Buda-Pesth. His principal army remaining concentrated, formed an imposing barrier, and had a great superiority over that of the insurgents; the marshal had imagined that, from this circumstance, and from the fact of the Magyars having made so slight a resistance to his advance, the insurrection would be completely put down by the occupation of the capital. This hope, indeed, was not without foundation; but although in fact, it might not be so, still it was inexplicable at the time, why the insurgents were allowed to re-assemble, and form, behind the Theiss, a new plan of operations. The Prince, perhaps, hesitated to commit his army to the extreme rigours of a winter campaign, beyond the Theiss. He well knew the hostile feelings of the inhabitants of Pesth, and, in fact, had not sufficient forces for the occupation of the city, and the continuation of such a formidable campaign; besides which, there is no doubt that he was cajoled into inaction by those insidious Hungarians, who still, outwardly, remained faithful to the Austrian cause.

The diet and revolutionary government of Hungary, on their retirement to Debreczin, strained every nerve to re-assure the failing spirits of their party, and they began to recover from their first alarm. They had taken with them the government bank-note press, and had a factory for the manufacture of muskets and arms, at Groswardein. They put the mills in requisition for the making of gunpowder; spies were distributed, as commissioners, throughout the counties; they decreed a levy, *en masse*, in all the provinces which were not subject to the imperial arms. Considerable reinforcements arrived from Poland, led by Dembinski; and the troops were disciplined and exercised by experienced officers; but their greatest resource was in their numerous adherents still remaining in the capital, by whose instrumentality they were always exactly informed of the plans projected for the future proceedings of the Austrian army.

Count Dembinski, whose name became celebrated during the revolution in Poland, in 1830, by his address and courage as one of the insurgent generals, is about sixty years of age; of a commanding appearance, being tall and well-built. Kossuth had invited him to join his standard, with the intention of making him commander-in-chief of the army of the Theiss; but, on a misunderstanding with Geörgey, he was obliged to be contented, for a time, with a rather subordinate command.

The diet now took possession of the crown and regalia of Hungary, and caused them to be transported to Groswardein, under a military escort, with great pomp. The Magyars attached a superstitious value to this crown. There is a legend that it was wrought by the hands of angels for St. Stephen, who was crowned with it in the year 1001. History, with a more limited faith, has recorded that it was sent as a present to Stephen, by Pope Sylvester the Second. In 1072 Duke Geisa received from the Greek emperor a golden circlet, or royal band, for his brow. When he was afterwards made King of Hungary, he joined this circlet to the diadem; so that the crown was composed of two kingly elements united. When the race of the Asseds became extinct, in 1301, there was a double election to the vacant throne. One party chose Robert of Anjou and Naples; the other, Wenzel the younger, of Bohemia: the cause of the latter, however, did not prosper, and his affairs had taken a very unfortunate turn, when his father, then King of Bohemia, marched an army to Ofen, and carried off his son, and the crown with him, to Prague. The Hungarians then definitively elected Otto, of Bavaria, and the King of Bohemia was induced to give up the crown to him. Otto, to take possession of his kingdom, had to pass through Austria, which he did *incognito*, carrying the crown with him. It was packed in a small cask, and hung at the saddle-bow of a German Baron, who discovered, one morning, that he had lost his precious charge during the previous night. The royal party had then arrived at Fishament, not far from Vienna; and were about to cross the Danube, but they now retraced their steps, and, by great good fortune, found cask and crown uninjured.

In the year 1307, Otto went to Siegenburgen, on a visit to the Waywode Lladislas, intending to gain him over, to espouse his cause; but the Waywode seized the crown and made the king a prisoner. After a short time, he set Otto free; but he retained possession of the diadem for three years; but, on threats of war, restored it. In 1439, on the decease of the Emperor Albrecht the Fourteenth, there was another double election; the two rivals for the crown being Wladislaw, of Poland, and Ladislas, the infant son of Albrecht. The widow of Albrecht resolved to have the child crowned; and for that purpose the diadem was purloined from the castle of Wissegrad, by one of her maids of honour. In 1441 the Empress pledged the crown to the Emperor Frederick the Fourth for two thousand five hundred florins; about two hundred and fifty pounds of our money. It was redeemed by Matthew Corvinus, and taken back to Wissegrad; and thence it was again stolen, in order to crown John Zapolya. He gave it in charge to Prenz, who delivered it to Ferdinand the First, and he was crowned with it in 1527; but it then fell into the hands of the Turks. As Solyman the Great returned from the siege of Vienna, he publicly exhibited the crown to his soldiers at Ofen. He sent it to his *protegé* Zapolya, on whose death it again got into possession of Ferdinand. Rudolph the Second sent the crown to Prague; Matthias the Second brought it back to Presburg, where, in 1619, it was seized by Gabor. He gave it up to Ferdinand the Second. The Emperor Joseph had it brought to Vienna. Leopold sent it back to Hungary; and it remained at Pesth until it was removed by the diet on their retreat to Debreczin.

By possession of the government bank-note press, Kossuth had an unlimited command of money, and it was put into constant requisition. Working day and night, for some time, he was enabled to emit an enormous quantity of notes; and a law having been passed by the diet, making it death for any party to refuse them, they soon became current throughout that part of the country. During the progress of the revolution, as much as sixty millions of florins (six million pounds of our money) were distributed in Hungary; and thousands of persons were entirely ruined who had these notes in their possession at the end of the war; for, of course, they were utterly valueless. It was a serious oversight, that the imperial authorities had omitted to decree formally and at once, the abolition of these revolutionary bank-notes, for it was therefore supposed that they were valid, and would be recognized, at any rate, some day by the government, whichever way the war might terminate. These formed the sinews of war, and enabled Kossuth to grasp enormous power and consideration. Immense *depôts* of arms from foreign countries, and provisions and equipments of war of all kinds, were created by these means. The new levies were well paid and exercised, and formed established regiments; and an energetic call to the spirit of the nation was responded to by the accession of a great number of Polish and German officers. The Magyars, informed by their spies and partizans in every part of the country of the motions of the imperial army, soon learned the fatal orders for isolated detachments being placed on the line of defence taken up by the Austrians, and having now procured an efficient army, they once more raised their heads, and resolved on taking the offensive.

After the surrender of Pesth, the Hungarian army had retired in two columns; one, under General Georgey, marched on Waitzen; the other, under Perczel, had gained the left bank of the Theiss, by Szolnok. This last column had been followed by a brigade of Austrian cavalry, under General Ottinger, which occupied Szolnok, while another brigade, forming the reserve, halted at Alberti.

Perczel, having received considerable reinforcements of honvéds from Debreczin and Grosswardein, speedily took the offensive; having crossed the Theiss, he succeeded in turning the position of General Ottinger. Obliged to retreat, the Austrian commander took up another defence at Czegled, where he awaited reinforcements. General Geörgey having attained Waitzen without molestation, took the bold resolution to carry the war into the rear of the Imperial army, by marching his corps toward Schemnitz; the whole of this part of the country being left unguarded by the Austrians, he was enabled to paralyze all aggressive operations that the Prince might have proposed in that quarter. Indeed, on the news of the expedition of General Geörgey reaching the Austrian quarters, a strong division under

General Czorich was sent to follow, and another column, commanded by General Görz, reinforced by a brigade from the troops of General Simunich, was ordered to oppose his march; but this plan did not succeed; for, by some accident or misunderstanding, these corps never became concentrated; and, although Czorich attacked the Magyars, and obtained a temporary advantage, Geörgey was enabled, by taking another direction, to wards Rosenberg, to compromise the detachment under Schlik, which was posted in this locality. General Schlik at this time was engaged in an enterprise on the Theiss. Having received the news of the victorious march of the Austrians, and the occupation of Pesth, he designed by this movement to aid in the successes of his countrymen. Leaving a brigade at Kaschau, he marched on to Szanto, and there united the remainder of his corps, with the intention of attacking the concentrated body of the insurgents near Tokay, under the command of Dembinski. But the Austrian general was not aware of the expedition of Geörgey, nor had he obtained any exact information as to the strength of the enemy he was about to attack.

A reconnoissance showed that the Magyars occupied an advantageous position not far from Tokay, at Tarczal and Keresztur, and Schlik determined on a general attack against these positions. The affair began in the midst of a thick fog, and was continued for a length of time with more or less success, and some hard fighting took place, the positions being taken and retaken several times during the day; but at length the Austrians found themselves overmatched, and the Magyars made them retreat with great loss to Tallya. Fortunately, a strong division had been detached from Pesth to the support of General Schlik, and it having joined, this brave general again commenced offensive operations against Tokay; but the insurgents had done enough; they offered no further resistance, and, after having exchanged shots, retired to the left bank of the Theiss. Schlik's intentions were to advance on Debreczin; but the division of Geörgey, before-mentioned, caused him not only to renounce his plan, but also to abandon his position. The latter general advanced on Eperies, to take the division of General Schlik in the rear, while Dembinski should attack him in front. Geörgey was enabled to form a junction with the corps under Dembinski; but the plan of a combined attack did not come off; for Schlik, having ascertained the extreme danger of his position, retired in all haste to Rima-Sombath, from which place he could either join the principal army, or unite himself to other Austrian brigades posted in that neighbourhood. The insurgents, having concentrated their forces, now crossed the Theiss, under the joint command of Geörgey and Dembinski, to the amount of fifty thousand men and one hundred and fifty pieces of ordnance, and menaced Pesth by taking the high road of Kaschau. Far from imagining that the insurgent chiefs had really taken the offensive, Prince Windishgrätz saw only in this movement an opportunity, not to be lost, of breaking the state of inactivity to which he had been condemned by the want of efficient succour from his government; and he resolved to offer a general battle.

The fortress of Leopoldstadt had surrendered at discretion, and the corps which had blockaded it was ordered to strengthen the troops near Comorn, which place was now closely invested.

In the south the Imperial arms had been crowned with success, through the combined efforts of the Servians, and the corps of Count Nugent. The insurgents in this part of the country, after two defeats, had fled in the direction of Peterwardein and Szegedin; these successes had allowed General Rukawina to succour Arad, which fortress the Magyars had attacked; and he chased them from the left bank of the Maros. The Austrians also attacked the insurgent chiefs Damianich, Vetter, and Gaal, and took their batteries by assault; at the same time, all the right banks of the Danube was in submission to the corps of Count Nugent. After having occupied the counties of Buranya and Sumigh, he appeared under the walls of Esseg, and, with the well-timed co-operation of General Trebersbourg, that fortress surrendered to their arms. At the moment, therefore, that the insurgents, under Geörgey and Dembinski, had crossed the Theiss, and were ready to act on the offensive, the general state of affairs appeared favourable to the Imperial cause.

Of the four fortresses which the insurgents possessed, two, Leopoldstadt and Esseg, were now in their occupation. Comorn and Peterwardein were both blockaded; the insurgents were cut off from the counties of the north—from the right bank of the Danube and from the Banat. They were masters on the north of the road from Kaschau, by Lozonz to Waitzen; and, on the south, with the exception of Szegedin, of the course of the Theiss and Maros. And, although the troops were immeasureably distended, yet they could, in a given time, concentrate themselves in masses at the north or south, and thus give intensity to their operations.

Prince Windishgrätz having left a portion of his forces to observe the passage of the Theiss and Szolnok, and to cover Pesth at this point, betook himself with the remainder to Gyöngyös, to combine with General Schlik an attack against the position which the insurgent army occupied, not far from Kapolna; and the plan decided on was, that while the marshal should attack in front, Schlik should appear by the defiles of Verpelet, and turn the left flank of the enemy; and a strong brigade should be ordered to precede the anticipated retreat of the insurgents to Poroszlo; by these manœuvres it was expected that the enemy would be thrown again on the Theiss; that they would then be received by their adversaries on the long dykes of Thissa Fured, and thus that a decisive victory would be obtained over them.

After severe fighting, during the whole of the 26th, 27th, and 28th of February, and the 1st of March, Prince Windishgrätz had succeeded in the above plan; and, on this latter day, the insurgents, favoured by a thick fog, retreated, and took the road to Poroszlo. The only thing, therefore, now that the Imperial army had to do, was to advance on this place, to throw the insurgents to the river, and the success of this movement would probably have been decisive of the war. But, for some extraordinary reasons, never explained, the execution of this latter disposition did not take place, and the enemy operated their retreat without being followed by the Austrians; and were enabled also to carry with them all their artillery and baggage. The prior successes of the Austrian army became therefore steril, and the principal body again remained in a state of inactivity. Prince Windishgrätz contented himself by maintaining an imposing defensive position, and appeared to wait the arrival of twenty thousand men, which had been promised him a long time, as a reinforcement to his army.

Comorn was continued to be closely invested; but the siege of the fortress was pursued very languidly. The insurgents profited by the apparent prostration and inactivity of the Austrian army, and organized their grand expedition; and they concealed their general plans by partial attacks on their enemy.

The Austrian brigade which occupied Szolnok was surprised in front and rear by fifteen thousand Magyars, who had crossed the Theiss without having been perceived, and nearly cut to pieces. It retired to Czegled. At the same time a large force under Damianich, Vetter, and Gaal, took the offensive near Arad, and General Bem carried everything before him. He beat and dispersed the Austrians in the north of Transylvania, and appeared before Hermannstadt, where General Puchner had posted himself with about four thousand men and eighteen cannon. And here this latter general obtained a signal victory, after a hard combat of seven hours; but his situation, notwithstanding a reinforcement he had received, became more perilous from day to day.

The Szeklers revolted in General Bem's favour, and joining themselves to a body from his army, rose in masses on all sides, and threatened Cronstadt and Hermannstadt. On the other side, a strong column arriving from Arad succeeded in completely interrupting all communication between Temesvar and the principal army of the Imperialists. The detachments in Transylvania were therefore entirely isolated.

In this state of things the inhabitants of Cronstadt and Hermannstadt renewed their demand for the Austrian general to obtain the assistance of Russian troops. General Puchner, convinced of his danger, convoked a council of war, and set forth the desire of the inhabitants. The council acceded to their wishes, and the Commander-in-chief of the Russian troops in Wallachia immediately sent two detachments to these cities. The Russian General Engelhardt occupied Cronstadt, and Colonel Scariatine entered Hermannstadt.

Bem now made an unsuccessful attack near Hermannstadt, and retired to Deva, after having destroyed the bridge across the Strelia; and a favourable turn seemed to open to the Imperial arms. The Russians saw an occasion to attack a strong body of the Szeklers, and totally defeated them; but these partial successes soon vanished. The heroic General Bem redoubled in activity after his failure, and having received an accession to his forces from the county of Zarand, obliged the Austrians to retreat from Mediasch, and took possession of it. Puchner, having concentrated his forces, attacked the insurgents; and although he beat them, this manœuvre left the road to Hermannstadt open. Bem seized the opportunity, and threw himself with rapidity on that city. Colonel Scariatine, who occupied it with two thousand five hundred men and eight pieces of cannon, informed Puchner of his situation, and prepared to defend himself—but it was in vain. While the Russian troops were occupied in resisting in front, masses of soldiers poured into the city at the rear, and Scariatine saw himself obliged to cut his way through the streets, and retired to the passage of the Rothenthurm; Pushner, finding that the insurgents had possession of the city, judged rightly that all was lost. His troops were completely worn out with fighting, and being still menaced by the enemy, he gave them *carte blanche* to make the best of their way to the frontiers of the principalities, by way of Cronstadt, and he himself retired into Wallachia. The Russian general, Engelhardt, finding himself alone at Cronstadt, also repassed the frontier, and thus the whole of Transylvania was lost to the Imperial arms.

Prince Windishgrätz had remained all this time passive in his positions before mentioned. Informed by their spies of the situation of the Austrians, the insurgent chiefs combined their plan of attack. They divided themselves into two columns, while General Klapka, at the head of one of them, with twenty thousand men and fifty pieces of cannon, was to debouch at Szolnok, and menace Pesth; the other column, containing fifty thousand men under General Georgey, should operate from Hatwan to Waitzen, throw back the Austrian detachments, and raise the siege of Comorn. General Schlik had to sustain the first attack of the enemy; very superior forces were opposed to him, and he was obliged to retire behind the river Zagywa. On this, Prince Windishgrätz sent him succour, and ordered the Ban Jellacic to establish a communication with the left wing of the principal army. He held a council of war at Aszod. After a long and anxious debate, the majority decided that Pesth should not be abandoned, and the army received the order to concentrate itself in the plains of Rakos, before that city. This was effected, although with great difficulty and some loss; and the army took up a position from Palotta by Kerestur and Soroksar, and thus made a lengthy incurvation. The communication with the corps of General Schlik was happily attained; but it was found that this new position, obtained with so much effort, did not in the least ameliorate their situation; the principal part of the army was obliged to remain stationary for the steril defence of Pesth; and the lengthened bend it took allowed the corps of Klapka alone to keep it in check. Georgey immediately hurried on with his force to Waitzen, where nothing could stand before him.

It was at this moment that the diet of Hungary, still sitting at Debreczin, proclaimed that Hungary, with Transylvania and the countries annexed to it, should be one free and independent state; that the House of Hapsburg-Lorraine should be for ever excluded from the government and exiled from the country; that the future form of government should be fixed at a later period by the national assembly; until that time Louis Kossuth should be president, and invested with all power, and that he should make choice of a ministry, who, with him, should undertake the direction of public affairs.

The government at Vienna was astounded at these prospects. After a war of five months the insurgents appeared in the field stronger than ever; and it was feared that by persevering in the system laid down by the Austrian commanders, a serious disaster would become inevitable. The ministry therefore thought it necessary to effect a total change in the disposition of the army; and this could only be done by removing the commander-in-chief; the necessity, however, appeared so urgent that they did not hesitate—they confided the army to General Weldon, and conferred on him the most extensive powers; and reinforcements, under General Wohlgemuth, were marched to the blockading corps before Comorn.

But these tardy measures could not stay the advance of the insurgents; after the occupation of Waitzen, General Georgey advanced in two columns, which attained, at the same time—the one by the left bank of the Grann, the other by that of Lewa—the three points of Kalna, Bars, and Saint Benedek. General Wohlgemuth, on his arrival at the scene of action, took position between Malas and Bese. Georgey, profiting by his numerical superiority, covered his centre with a weak curtain, and manœuvred with two strong columns by Nagy-Sarlo and Verebeley on the two wings of General Wohlgemuth: this clever movement succeeded admirably; and, after a short resistance, General Wohlgemuth was forced to retire behind the Neutra. The enterprise of Geörgey fully succeeded; the blockade of Comorn was raised between the Waag and the Danube, the insurgents were enabled to communicate with the garrison then under Guyon, and they, in conjunction with Georgey, took the offensive, and successfully drove the enemy away.

General Weldon at once perceived the extreme danger of continuing the prolonged occupation of Pesth, in the presence of the rapid progress of Georgey on the left bank of the Danube. The insurgents had assembled considerable forces in the south of Hungary, and had proceeded aggressively. Arad was summoned; the fortress of Temesvar could only keep the defensive, and the Servians had been thrown back upon the Danube; the isolated detachments of Mamula and Nugent were menaced with destruction, and the frontiers of the Servian country and those of Croatia remained exposed to the incursions of the insurgents. General Weldon, seeing that it was impossible to hold Pesth, decided on retreating at once, and concentrating his forces rapidly towards Presburg and Esseg; for he had fears of an invasion of the Austrian territory by the enemy under Georgey. Nevertheless it was decided (although not with his concurrence individually) that the fortress of Ofen should still be held by the Imperialists, and its defence was confided to General Hentzi, with a strong garrison and provisions for two months.

The Ban descended the Danube to protect the menaced frontiers of Servia, Sclavonia and Croatia; the remainder of the Austrian army, thrown back on both sides of the Danube by the march of the enemy on Waitzen and Grann, and subsequent reverses, could only reunite itself at Presburg; thus broken it offered no resistance to the enemy—it abandoned the lines of the Waag and of the Raab—it retired from the siege of Comorn, and quitted the whole of the previously occupied country, to group itself in a defensive position round Presburg, drawing in as close as possible its positions at Tyrnau, near the lake of Neusiedel.

CHAPTER V.

It was admitted by all parties at Vienna, that just before the position of affairs in Hungary had so unexpectedly changed, Austria had reason to congratulate herself on her situation; the very name of Prince Schwarzenberg had inspired the Viennese with a wholesome fear, and, coupled with that of General Weldon as Military Commandant of the city, had kept the people on their good behaviour. It was true that for each man condemned by court martial for participation in the insurrection and shot, the life of a sentinel was attempted, and not all the stringent orders of the commandant, or the strictest investigations of the police, could effect any discovery of the offenders; but beyond this species of vengeance, the people were quiet—the order for the delivery up of arms, and the search in all houses by the military for that purpose, had produced a large quantity; but it was known that immense numbers of muskets had been buried in the various gardens and courtyards of houses in the suburbs, in the hope that they might at some future time be again of service.

Soon after the resumption of the sittings of the diet at Kremsier, to which place about two hundred and forty-eight deputies had arrived, that body applied itself to the formation of the new charter, and began its labours by laying down fundamental principles; the first of which, voted by a large majority, was to the effect "that all power emanated from the people." This principle was combatted by the ministry, and Count Stadion, who was minister of the interior, protested against its adoption; he argued that in the particular case of Austria this principle was inadmissible, for in the month of March, 1848, the Emperor Ferdinand had consented, of his own free will, to grant a constitution to his subjects, and to divide the legislative power descended to him from his ancestors, without any restrictions whatever, with their representatives; it was granted that, by this concession, Austria had entered into the rank of constitutional states, but this fact did not abolish the form of the monarchical state, nor impede its vigour; it was shown, moreover, that the inviolability of the monarchical principle had been maintained throughout all the Imperial decrees and proclamations published since March, 1848, and most particularly in the decree of the 16th of May, in that year, which contained the imperial resolution to submit the charter of the constitution of the 15th of April to the deliberation of the representatives of the people, and by which decree the first diet was declared legally constituted; it was, therefore, in the division of the legislative power, between the monarch and the representatives of the people, that the ministry understood a constitutional political condition, and therefore that the pretension "that all power emanated from the people," was incompatible with the fundamental condition of the monarchy. This protest was met by a decision of the diet, of a hundred and ninety-six voices against ninety-nine, that the adoption of this reasoning would fetter their liberty of action, and that was incompatible with the dignity of a constitutional assembly! Nevertheless, two days later, the above argument of the minister seems to have had its weight, for this same "first principle" was rejected by the assembly, when again called on for its decision. Instead of proceeding practically, the members of this diet occupied themselves with theoretical discussions on subjects entirely unconnected with the formation of the charter; they meddled with every act of ministers, and were most incessant in questioning them on every report they had heard, as to the general progress of the affairs of the country; and in a short time it was discovered that some of them were in active correspondence with the leading men of the revolution in Hungary, and intriguing in their interest. So open indeed were their acts, that they subjected themselves to a charge of high treason; the diet also proceeded to abolish all titles and privileges of nobility, and it put forth such preposterous pretensions, that the ministry found it impossible to carry on the government in the face of them. Prince Schwarzenberg was thoroughly disgusted; and, seeing that no real progress was made in the formation of the constitutional laws, he at once determined to bring forward a measure himself, and on the 4th of March, 1849, the charter, which had been for some time in preparation by him, in anticipation of the inability of the diet, was published to that body and to the country at large. It appeared under the form of a patent emanating from the Emperor, and was introduced by the Prince with the assertions that when the late Emperor Ferdinand, of his own free will, agreed to grant liberal institutions to his subjects, gratitude and joy were visible throughout the country, but that ulterior events had not justified the hope then raised—that internal peace had vanished—that poverty had menaced the country, lately blessed with so much of abundance—that secret conspiracies of discontented persons still exacted an exceptional state to be kept up in the capital of Vienna—that civil war was devastating one part of the kingdom, while in another an actual state of warfare hindered the introduction of regulated institutions—that though exterior repose was undisturbed, yet discord and defiance had found many adherents—that this state of things was the abuse, not the use of true liberty, and that it was the duty of the Emperor to put down all disorder and revolution—that in the manifesto of the 2nd of December, the Emperor had pronounced the hope that, with the blessing of God, and the intelligence of his people, he should succeed in uniting all the countries and nations forming the monarchy into one grand political body—that this desire had been well received everywhere, for it was the expression of a want felt for a long time by the general body of the people—

that it was in the renewal of the common monarchy, in the strict union of its several parts, that the good sense of the people would acknowledge the first condition for the restoration of order, and for the return of prosperity—but that the diet, convoked by the late Emperor, had occupied itself in attempting to form a constitution for a portion only of the monarchy—that the ministry had resolved, notwithstanding the equivocal conduct of that body, on the 6th of October, at Vienna, to confide the ulterior execution of this great work to them, but that after several months of discussion it was perceived that nothing definite was settled—that their time was filled with discussions, not only in direct opposition to the laws and institutions of the country, but also contrary to the development of all improvement and civilization; and that the Emperor, therefore, of his own free will and power, had decided on granting a new charter for the whole monarchy—for Austria, one and indivisible.

This patent was divided into sixteen sections, and which treated of, 1st. The Empire. 2nd. The Emperor. 3rd. The rights of citizens in the Empire. 4th. The Communes, or provinces. 5th. The general affairs of each country. 6th. The general affairs of the Empire. 7th. The legislative power (exercised, for the general affairs in the empire, in concert with the diet of the empire—for the general affairs of each country in concert with the Austrian diet). 8th. The diet—a superior chamber composed of deputies elected for each country of the monarchy, by the members of the diet of the country which they would represent;—an inferior chamber, composed of deputies elected in the ordinary way, either on the principle of a census, or a personal right; for every hundred thousand men one deputy to be named. 9th. The constitution of each country and diets (all the constitutions of the particular states of the crown being in full action in the year 1849). 10th. Executive power. 11th. The council of the empire, being a consulting power. 12th. Judicial power. 13th. The tribunal of the Empire. 14th. The finances. 15th. The armed force. And, 16th. General dispositions and explanations. The Emperor at the same time promulgated a law, for indemnification in respect of the abolition of the robot (personal service of the peasants), or socage service

When this patent was read to the diet, that assembly was declared dissolved ; but the spirit of radicalism, and even of revolution, had been carried to such a pitch by some of its members, supported by a clique of agitators out of doors, that the ministry found it necessary to take precautions, when the Constitutional Charter was made public, and the diet actually dissolved ; it was the intention of ministers to have caused the arrest of these unruly members immediately after the dissolution; for this purpose, early in the morning of the 7th of March, a considerable body of troops was posted round the Archi-episcopal palace, where the diet held its sittings; the doors were occupied, and a large number of deputies were in their places, but the most obnoxious of them had divined that something of the kind was in preparation, and made their escape the evening before.

The dissolution of the diet, therefore, passed off quietly, and each of the members having received from the public exchequer, their expenses for the journey home, proportioned to the distance they had to go, made instant preparations to depart, and in a couple of days Kremsier was restored to its usual obscurity and insignificance; the pay of each member of the diet was two hundred florins a month.

This mischievous body having been

finally disposed of, the ministry was enabled to turn its attention more exclusively to the affairs of the nation,—and, indeed their time was fully occupied; for as we have seen, the affairs of Hungary were in a critical state, and unsatisfactory news arrived every day from the Lombardo-Venetian kingdom. Venice still held out, although reduced to great extremities from the blockade by sea and land of the Austrians; and now, on the 12th of March, Charles Albert denounced the armistice on the part of Piedmont, and declared that hostilities should recommence at the expiration of eight days. This prince thought himself in a condition to make head once more against the Austrians; the reorganization of his army had been confided to his generals, and it now amounted to sixty thousand choice troops. In answer to the call of influential persons, who demanded that new officers should command it, he had fixed his choice on

Generals Chrzanowski, a distinguished Polish general, and Romarino, (a Piedmontese officer of well known experience); but it was soon asserted that neither of these generals possessed the confidence of the army. The Lombards, who had fled to Piedmont, had been organized as a separate legion, and placed under the orders of General Romarino; but as far as concerned the arming of the country, scarcely were the strongholds in a good state of defence, the national guard was but half equipped, and the open country without protection.

Instead of combining this second aggression in Lombardy with "United Italy," Charles Albert and his government contented themselves with sending agents to Florence and Rome, and without waiting for their return, denounced the armistice, so that the new campaign began before a single man could push forward from those states to their support. Nevertheless, the cities of Lombardy and those of the Venetian territory were ready to rise on the first intimation of the invasion of the country by Charles Albert; and it was on this that he appeared to have placed his chief reliance for continuing the warfare. It was strongly asserted that the Austrian army would have been gravely compromised, if more popular commanders had had the direction of the Sardinian troops. It was known, however, that Chrzanowski was fettered and checked in all his propositions and plans, and General Romarino did not show the talents essentially necessary on so mighty an occasion. The principal support of the Sardinian army was to be looked for in the simultaneous rising of the people of Lombardy and the Venetian territory; it was therefore evident that the Piedmontese should have invaded Lombardy at once; but Charles Albert miscalculated the talents and activity of

Radetzky, and the spirit of the Austrians, and had no idea of being himself attacked before he entered the country in possession of his enemy. Radetzky understood his position so well, and saw so clearly the danger he ran by being taken between the Piedmontese army and the Lombard insurrection, that to avoid it he conceived the bold plan of carrying the war into the enemy's country.

Charles Albert had published a manifesto on the 15th of the month, addressed to the people of Europe, in which he stated that the causes of the renewal of the war were the violation of the stipulations of the armistice by the Austrians; their refusal to deliver up the park of artillery at Peschiera; their continued occupation of the Duchies; the blockade of Venice, and their vexatious conduct towards the inhabitants of those districts evacuated by the Sardinians; and he sent a herald to Radetzky, to propose that he, with his army, should retire behind the Oglio; but the Marshal's only answer was, that Austria would dictate terms of peace at Turin!

Radetzky published an order notifying to his troops the cessation of the armistice, and promising them that the new campaign should be short and decisive, and that they should find a lasting peace at Turin. He immediately made the most extensive preparations to meet the enemy; he ordered the reserve artillery corps and some battalions of infantry to Crema. His quarter-general and the first corps of his army marched to Melegnano, and this movement had the effect of deceiving Charles Albert, who supposed that the Austrians were about to retreat; but on the second day's march, the left flank of the army wheeled to the right, and the whole army concentrated itself at Pavia, two bridges were thrown over the Ticino, and the army passed over at several points, and advanced in three columns on the road of Galasco. The right column attained Zerbolo; the centre, Gropello; and the third, Dorno. The Piedmontese had but few outposts on the Ticino, and the right flank of their army, under the Duke of Genoa, made a movement to retire to the line of Vigevano and Montara. At the same time that the Austrians passed the Ticino, the fourth division of the Piedmontese army crossed the same river by the bridge of Buffalora, and advanced as far as Magenta, and Charles Albert established his quarter-general at Trecate. On the 21st, the Austrian army, being still divided into three columns, continued their advance; the left column from Dorno marched towards Montara, the centre from Gropello to Gambolo; and the right column from Zerbolo towards Vigevano, where, on its arrival, it came in contact with the Piedmontese, under the Duke of Genoa. After some hard fighting the Austrians remained masters of the ground; the centre column also gained considerable advantages over their enemy at Gambolo, and the left column, having marched directly towards Montara, a bloody battle here ensued. General d'Aspre, immediately on his arrival before this city, had stationed eighteen cannon, and commenced firing against the walls, and as soon as daylight appeared on the following morning, a strong division was advanced to the attack in seven columns, the artillery being ranged between them; the smoke from the incessant cannonade, and the nature of the ground, concealed this advance from the Piedmontese; the fire from their cannon was, however, of a fearful character, but this mode of warfare soon ceased, for the Austrians, pushing on, attacked their enemy with the bayonet. Montara was taken by assault, and many officers, men, and munitions of war, and all the equipage of the Duke of Savoy, fell into the hands of the Austrians, as prizes for their bold and successful attempt.

It was supposed that the Piedmontese had retired to Vercelle, and the main part of the Austrian army advanced in the direction of Novara, so as to manœuvre in either direction if necessary; but the former, having had their line of retreat cut by the loss of Montara, resolved to try their fortune by a pitched battle in the plains of Olenzo, before Novara. They had a strength of fifty thousand men, and the disposition of their troops was thus:—the first division, under General Durando, behind Corte-Nuova, to the left of the road of Vercelli; the second division, behind the farm of Cittadella; the third division, under General Perrone, near the church of Bicocca; the reserve corps, under the Duke of Genoa, at the cemetery of St. Nazzaro; the guards, under the Duke of Savoy, supported the right wing.

The second column of the Austrian army, forming the advanced guard, and which had the day before marched under the command of General d'Aspre, from Vespolate to Olengo, there met the Piedmontese force, which was posted on the heights. The battle immediately took place; and the resistance of the Piedmontese was such, that it was, for a length of time, doubtful which party would obtain the victory; but the first column of the Austrian army, advancing to the support of General d'Aspre, changed that doubt into a certainty in favour of the Austrians; and more particularly as Radetzky had posted a fourth column of the army in the right flank of the Piedmontese. The attacks of the Piedmontese were continued with great bravery, for many hours; but the Austrians, under the Archduke Albert (son of the late Archduke Charles), and General d'Aspre, gallantly maintained their front until the fourth column, having manœuvered successfully, on the other side of the Agogna, against the right flank of the Piedmontese, made its appearance. Radetzky, seizing this favourable moment, advanced with his reserve force, and a number of cannon clearing the way before him, the Marshal gave the order for a simultaneous advance of the whole army. The Piedmontese were obliged to retire on all points, and retreated to the mountains on the northern side.

The battle lasted from ten o'clock in the morning until late at night. This signal victory was obtained by the Austrians, with very considerable losses. Their trophies consisted of twelve cannon and a flag. Between two and three thousand prisoners were taken, besides which the Piedmontese lost two generals, sixteen officers, and nearly four thousand men.

Immediately after the battle was over, a herald sent by Charles Albert arrived on the field, to propose an armistice, and demanded a cessation of hostilities until the king could communicate with the chambers at Turin. This proposition was rejected, the Austrian commander declaring that hostilities should be continued night and day. Charles Albert now saw the necessity of taking some very decided step, and he at once abdicated the throne in favour of his son, the Duke of Savoy. Negociations were resumed; and on the 26th, an armistice was concluded between the belligerent parties, the conditions of which were, that the king should take immediate measures to secure a lasting peace between the two countries; that the portion of the Piedmontese army, formed by the Lombards, Hungarians, and Poles, (being subjects of the Emperor, and whose pardon for having joined the Piedmontese cause, Marshal Radetzky undertook to endeavour to obtain,) should be disbanded; that the Austrians should, during the armistice, occupy the territory between the Po, the Sesia, and the Ticino, as well as a moiety of the city of Alessandria and the citadel; that the Sardinian troops should quit possession of the territory of Parma, Modena and Tuscany; that the Sardinian fleet should leave the Adriatic; that their troops should quit Venice; and that the Sardinian army should be reduced to a peace establishment.

The Piedmontese attributed their disaster, in a great measure, to the conduct of General Romarino. They stated that this general, who was at the head of the Lombard division, had been charged with the defence of the river Ticino; that instead of advancing against the enemy with the whole of his force, (and which was most eager for battle,) when they prepared to cross the river, he allowed one of his battalions and a regiment of the line, to be almost crushed for want of assistance; and not satisfied with this culpable negligence, he did not notify to the Commander-in-chief that the passage of the Ticino had been forced. And this conduct, it was stated, was without doubt, the first cause of the fatal issue of the campaign; for when the Austrians had thus passed the Ticino, they succeeded in cutting the Sardinian army into two parts. General Romarino paid dearly for his conduct, for he was soon afterwards tried by a military tribunal, found guilty, and sentenced to death. Great influence was used to procure a respite — but in vain; he was shot a few days after the sentence had been pronounced.

On the 29th Radetzky returned to Milan in triumph, having, indeed performed to the letter, the promise in his general order, "that the campaign should be short but decisive." But before the final termination of hostilities in this part of the Austrian dominions, the most lamentable events took place at Brescia.

In consequence of false reports as to the terms of the armistice entered into between the Austrians and Piedmontese, by one of the articles of which it was reported that the Piedmontese should immediately evacuate the whole of Lombardy, a Committee of Defence was hastily formed at Brescia, whose first act was to call all its inhabitants to arms—barricades sprung up throughout the city, and the country people flocked by thousands in answer to the call—and the Committee prepared to defend the city against all aggressors. General Nugent, with a brigade of two thousand four hundred men, had posted himself at some distance from the city, and soon afterwards a body of troops detached from the second corps of the Austrian army arrived, to co-operate in quelling this mad insurrection. They soon intercepted all communication between the city and surrounding country; and the town was duly summoned to surrender. Deputations demanded a delay, which was accorded; but, instead of a peaceful answer, all the bells of the churches rang an alarm, and from the steeples, towers, roofs of houses and windows in the neighbourhood of the citadel, (which was garrisoned by Austrians) a murderous fire was directed against it. A short delay was still accorded to the inhabitants, under the impression that some misapprehension or mistake had caused this outbreak; but this pause producing no effect, a bombardment and assault of the city were ordered to take place simultaneously. A bloody battle soon took place in the streets, and the people defended themselves with great resolution from barricade to barricade, and from street to street. But the troops succeeded in gaining possession of part of the town, although with great loss; they fought until night stopped further devastation. By daylight the next morning the combat was renewed, and a most rigorous bombardment ordered. No more quarter was asked or given on either side, and the most horrible and sanguinary scenes took place; the houses, whence the inhabitants continued to pour forth their volleys, were all in flames, and the whole city seemed like a lake of fire. The troops could only advance step by step, fighting every inch of their way, each minute thinning their ranks, and themselves causing death and devastation to increase in intensity. But further assistance arriving to the Austrians, it was impossible for the city to hold out much longer; the greater part of the defenders, however, continued the sanguinary conflict to the last, and died sword in hand. At length, those remaining flew to the walls of the city, hoping thence to escape to the open country; but there they were received on the bayonets of their lately arrived assailants.

The combat had lasted from half-past three in the afternoon of the 31st of March until five o'clock in the evening of the 1st of April, when the city was militarily occupied by the Austrians. Brescia was, indeed, dreadfully punished for this fatal rising, and a thousand persons, at the least, found a horrible death in consequence.

CHAPTER VI.

The Magyar insurrection was nearly successful on all points. The Imperial flag waved only on the fortresses or forts of Ofen, Arad, Temesvar, Karlstadt and Deva. The two most important fortresses, Comorn and Peterwardein, protected and covered the whole country in possession of the insurgents; the first, the western provinces; the last, the southern parts. At the north, the chain of the Carpathians formed a natural defence ; and, occupied by a few troops only, could be maintained against any enemy.

Enthusiastic Hungary, under the impulses of fanaticism and terror, had accomplished the greatest efforts; twenty battalions of well-disciplined troops, one hundred and seventeen battalions of honveds (peasants who had served their military time, and were called out only to defend the country from invasion) ; sixteen regiments of cavalry, composed of foreign adventurers, German and Polish democrats, and eight hundred pieces of cannon, forming a grand total of one hundred and ninety thousand men, without counting irregulars, composed the enormous resources of this extraordinary insurrection. By the act of the diet of Hungary, of the 14th of April, which declared that the family of Hapsburg-Lorraine had ceased to reign in that country, and was excluded for ever from the throne, and which, in fact, established the republic, (although that form of government had not been openly proclaimed,) Kossuth and his party had cast away that false display of loyalty, by means of which he had so long deluded the nation. The revolutionary government thought itself strong enough to discard all ideas of a pacific tendency, and Kossuth, as dictator, reigned by terror, and conducted affairs as he chose; he had seized all the gold and silver of the country, which he substituted with his notes. It was stated broadly that, at this time he had twenty millions of florins in precious metals in his coffers! Such were the resources of the insurrection, and such the enemy that Austria had to cope with, at a time when the general situation of affairs elsewhere called for a great show of military strength. In short, the denunciation of the armistice by Charles Albert, the insurrections at Rome (which had just taken place) and in Tuscany—the prolonged resistance of Venice—the menacing attitude of the whole of northern Germany, and the revolutionary elements in the interior of the Austrian monarchy, subdued indeed, but not effectually put down, the present position of the Magyar army, and the gigantic scale of the insurrection—all these combined, caused the greatest alarm to the Austrian ministry, for the safety of the kingdom itself, and the probability of an invasion of the Austrian soil by the Magyars was now pressed strongly on the conviction of government; and it was thought that if the Magyar chiefs had better profited by the advantages at this moment in their power, and had taken a vigorous offensive position—if they had boldly passed the Austrian frontier and menacèd Vienna (where four-fifths of the population would have received them with acclamation and open arms), the situation of the monarchy would have been perilous in the extreme.

The public prints had for some time spoken of succour arriving from Russia; but nothing official was known on this head, until two proclamations, one from the Emperor of Austria, the other from the Emperor Nicholas, re-assured the public mind in announcing that Russia, quitting her passive attitude, was about to throw her strength into the scale for the maintenance of the Empire of Austria; and, almost at the same time, that is, about the 10th of May, the young Emperor of Austria gave signal proof of his devotion and courage, by resolving to join his armies personally, and fight his own battles for the salvation of his empire! It was a matter of great surprise to the Austrians, to see the Magyar army so long in a state of inactivity; but it soon transpired that a great part of it, commanded by Geörgey, had left the neighbourhood of Comorn, to besiege Ofen,—that thirty thousand men had been detached, for the attack of this important fortress. This was considered the great blunder of the insurgents; for, during the time occupied by the march and siege, the Austrians were enabled, in a great measure, to recover themselves, and the Russian army had had time to put itself in motion, to add their powerful assistance to the energetic campaign now resolved upon.

The garrison of Ofen was posted in the following manner: the third battalion of the regiment named Wilhelm occupied the trenches near the lower aqueduct; the third battalion of the military frontier of Warasdin held the higher aqueduct, and each of these battalions had five pieces of artillery; the battalion of Ceccopieri (an Italian regiment), and one from the Banat, occupied the inner fortress, on the ramparts of which were seventy-five cannon of large calibre. Geörgey had his quarter-general at Schwabenberg; the corps of Nagy-Sandor and of General

Aulich occupied Blocksburg, and spread to the right and behind the heights; the corps of Kmety and Knesier encamped round Leopoldfeld, and the surrounding heights were observed by hussars. On the 4th of May, Geörgey summoned the place to surrender; but General Hentzi, the brave defender of this fortress, pointed only to his flag. On the same day, the insurgents opened their first fire against the place, and harassed the besieged by false attacks. Hentzi, on his part, perceiving the destructive effect of the enemy's fire, opened a bombardment on the city of Pesth, situated opposite to him, on the other side of the Danube. He began the cannonade on the 13th at seven in the evening, and continued it till midnight; and, during the whole of this time, the Magyars threw shells and rockets into the fortress of Ofen. Hentzi made vigorous sorties from day to day; but, notwithstanding this, the insurgents were enabled to erect a breaching battery on the Spitzberg, and succeeded in making a breach, near the gate of Stuhlweissenberg. Hentzi did all that a brave soldier could do to sustain the courage of the garrison, but the decisive moment approached. Geörgey, after having, on the 19th and 20th, executed two false attacks, commanded an incessant fire from his guns during the whole of the night of the 21st; and at four on the following morning ordered the general attack; the insurgent columns assaulted the ramparts on all points, and succeeded in escalading them at the side near the gates of Stuhlweissenberg and Vienna. Perceiving that the garrison of the inner fortress was too weak of itself to resist the assailing masses, Hentzi called in two companies of the battalion of Wilhelm from the aqueduct; but at the moment these companies arrived on the spot where they were ordered, the compact columns of the insurgents appeared also. Hentzi attacked them bravely; but his weak band was overpowered, and he himself fell mortally wounded.

During this time, the commanding officer of the four companies remaining near the aqueducts, seeing the great danger which menaced the higher fortifications, rushed to the assistance of their brethren in arms; but two of these found the roads leading to the fortress already in possession of the enemy, and could not advance; their brave officers were all slain at the head of their soldiers, and a dreadful carnage ensued. The two other companies entered the fortress at the moment when the garrison, engaged in fighting their way through the streets, were retreating towards their barracks. Their colonel could not bear the idea of surviving this disgrace, and, rushing to a powder magazine, blew himself and all those around him into the air! Thus fell the fortress of Ofen, the loss of which made a deep impression on the Austrian Commander-in-chief; for it was perceived that Geörgey, having thirty thousand additional troops at command, might order them on the Waag and march direct for Presburg. Compelled to make head against the enemy on both sides of the Danube, the Austrian army was in no position or strength to resist a well-combined attack, and the Commander-in-chief began to feel the most serious forebodings, when, most opportunely and fortunate for the Austrian cause, a division of the Russian army, amounting to sixteen battalions and forty-eight pieces of artillery, commanded by General Paniutine, arrived by rail from the North, and took up a position at Hradisch, on the west side of the Carpathian mountains not far from the frontiers of Hungary.

Prince Paskiewitsch, having been informed of the perilous position of the

Austrians, had taken on himself the responsibility of acceding to the urgent request of the government, and had ordered this movement. The arrival of this division changed the aspect of affairs. Any aggressive movement on the part of Geörgey could now be met effectively, and the Austrian army had time to re-organize itself. General Welden, whose health had been completely worn by his late energetic attempts to reform the army, having quitted his command, the government nominated General Haynau to the post. The plan of operations, combined by the two cabinets of Austria and Russia, was that a Russian army should be concentrated at Dukla in Gallicia, and penetrate into Hungary by the Carpathians; that a second auxiliary Russian corps should march from Wallachia in Transylvania, under the command of General Lüders. and be seconded in its operations by another Russian column, which should act from Bucowina on

Bistritz, and be assisted by the Austrian corps of General Clamm, composed of the remaining part of the corps of General Puchner; and that the principal Austrian forces, reinforced by the Russian division under General Paniutine, should form the third column; that a separate detachment, under General Grabbe, should operate in the valley of the Waag and on the plain of Schemmitz, and bind the operations of the two principal armies.

Prince Paskiewitsch took the chief command of the Russian troops, and that of the Austrians was confided to General Haynau. This combination demanded time to execute, but there was little to spare; for the affairs in the south of Hungary had taken a deplorable turn for the Austrian cause, ever since the retreat of the Imperial army from Pesth. The insurgents, having an imposing force in this part of the country, easily routed the feeble corps which had been left to act there separately.

On the 22nd of March, the insurgents had appeared in great strength before Arad, and this fortress was strictly blockaded and reduced to a most desperate condition. In the Banat, General Rukawina had been compelled to shut himself up in a stronghold, and his situation became day by day more precarious. On the frontiers of Servia, the insurgents had made great progress. General Puffer had retired to Carlowitz with scarcely three thousand men; Meyerhofer held Semlin with but twelve hundred men; Mamula watched Peterwardein. But separated thus, what could the Austrians do against the combined force of the insurgents?—indeed, an invasion from them was daily expected into the military district of the battalion of the Czaikistes, which was the kernel of Servia; but Stratimirowitsch, with a body of troops hastily levied, and Colonel Knizanin, with the auxiliary troops of Turkish Servia, which had been called on, in aid, succeeded in repelling an attempt at invasion of this district, and they were assisted by the opportune arrival of the Ban at Essek, with his corps; and this latter general, by dint of great energy and perseverance, was able to reform and complete the ranks of his army, thinned as well by sickness, as by repeated attacks of the enemy. The Ban was soon, however, strong enough to make head against the insurgents; and he took up a position between Kacs and Jarek, along the Roman rampart, with the intention of attacking his enemy, and throwing him back to the canal of Baczka. The Magyar forces, nothing daunted, soon offered battle. and drew up a formidable line of artillery against the camp at Kacs; but they were unsuccessful in their attempt, and were obliged to retreat with great loss. One of their battalions of honveds, being surrounded, was actually cut in pieces. The Ban marched on Neusatz, and notwithstanding the continued fire from the neighbouring fortress of Peterwardein, succeeded in taking the town by storm. By these successes the Ban obtained a strong defensive position along the length of the canal of Baczka, and the commanding points of the passage of Verbas and St. Thomas; but he already foresaw that his indefatigable enemy would soon return in greater numbers, and did not dissemble his anxieties at head-quarters; but there was no assistance to be rendered him at the moment, and he remained in a most precarious condition.

The Commander-in chief, General Haynau, now ordered different movements of the corps stationed on the left bank of the Danube, to cause their gradual approach to this river, so as to concentrate them on the right bank at the earliest intimation. The insurgents, at the same moment, meditated an irruption on the left bank. They had re-established the bridges on the Waag, at Nagya and Sereg-Akol, and menaced the right bank of this river. On the 17th of June they appeared in great strength over the Waag, at Negyed, and, a few days later, successfully attacked General Pott at Zsigard, who retreated. The Russian division, under General Paniutine, came up, however, and on the next day the combined force resolved on an attempt to beat back the enemy. At this aspect of affairs the insurgents retired on Kiraly-Rew and Pered, and took up a position between this village and Deaky. After a hard battle, the combined forces compelled the insurgents to retire on the whole of their line, and they retreated to the left bank of the Waag.

This was a very unfortunate issue for the Hungarian cause; for, in fact, Georgey (who commanded), in attacking the allied army on the Waag, at a moment when they had partially succeeded in operating a concentration of their forces on the right bank of the Danube, had the plan to frustrate this concentrative movement by menacing Presburg; and, by assembling an enormous force on the Raab, he hoped to disguise his views. But this double combination having completely failed, caused him very sensible loss, and, above all, produced a disastrous moral effect on the whole of his army, by proving that the Russian intervention was for them a sad reality. The principal Russian army had now concentrated itself at Dukla; at which place the Emperor Nicholas came and passed them in review.

By the 17th of June the Russian troops had penetrated into Hungary, in several columns. The third corps, from which the division, under General Paniutine, had been detached near the Austrian army, marched under the command of General Rüdiger by Neumark, Ofal, and Toliberg, upon the Lublo. The second corps, under General Kuprianof, one of whose divisions operated, in conjunction with that of the Austrian under General Grabbe, in the valley of the Waag and of the Arwa, was directed towards Izbe and Konieczno. The fourth corps, whose commander was General Tcheodajeff, one of whose divisions covered Bucowina, received orders to proceed to Zmigrod to Graab, and from Dukla to Komornik.

Prince Paskiewitsch had his quarter-general at Szincino. A simultaneous advance was made, and the Magyars retired in divers places, evacuating Eperies. General Tcheodajeff followed closely, and caused them still to retire as far as the gates of Tarcsa, where their reserve was posted. On the 24th of June, Prince Paskiewitsch made his dispositions to attack Budimer, and it was expected that a general battle would have ensued; but the Magyars avoided the combat, abandoned Budimer as well as Kaschau, and retired by Hidas-Nemethy, on Miskolcz. At Kaschau the Prince halted, to await intelligence of the operations of General Grabbe.

The third corps, with General Rüdiger, quitted Eperies and advanced to Kaschau. The second corps was directed towards Hidas-Nemethy, and there took up position. Being thus master of the line of the Sajo, Prince Paskiewitsch projected and carried into execution an advance to the other side of the Theiss, as far as Debreczin. General Tcheodajeff was intrusted with this expedition, which signally succeeded; for Debreczin surrendered without striking a blow. While the Russian army thus penetrated into the heart of Hungary, almost without resistance, General Grabbe accomplished his mission. The Cossacks attached to the Austrian division were obliged to swim over the Waag—for the Magyars, in retiring, had destroyed the bridge near Rosenberg; and they marched towards the plain of Schemnitz.

But the Magyars, on their side, pursued the siege of Arad and Temesvar with great activity; the first named fortress, having been reduced to great extremities, had capitulated, and this stronghold was converted into a depôt for their munitions of war and provisions; but Temesvar, although sorely pressed, had not yet hauled down its flag. The Magyar corps under Perczel had been reinforced by the garrison of Szegedin and Thérésiopel, and, with other corps, took the offensive with the view of a decisive attack against the army of the south; but the Ban, anticipating this, attacked Perczel before he could concentrate his forces. He marched resolutely on Kis-Hegyes, but he had miscalculated his strength, for here he met with the most obstinate resistance, and eighty pieces of artillery being opened against him, he found he had been grossly deceived by his spies; in this critical position, however, by clever manœuvres, he saved his army from destruction, and was enabled to retreat without very great loss; but his post at the canal of Baczka was no longer tenable, and he crossed the Danube at Titel, still, however, continuing the blockade of Peterwardein.

The affairs of the south would now have been desperate for the Austrian cause if General Haynau, having received information of the successful advance of the Russians in the north, had not himself taken the offensive; but the Magyars were now in immense strength, and had resolved "to stand the hazard of the die." The whole force of the insurrection (with the exception of twelve thousand men, who were in the Marmarosch, and of twenty-five thousand defending Transylvania) amounted to one hundred and fifty thousand! and were all available on the Danube and Theiss, and could, in a short space of time, be concentrated for any given operations.

This enormous army, it was supposed, by operating cleverly in the centre between two armies separated by an immense tract of country, and having for support the two important fortresses of Comorn and Peterwardein, might have caused the greatest difficulties to the combined forces of Russia and Austria; but, unfortunately for them, the Magyars were for some time doubtful of the fact of the active participation of the Russians in the war, and they neglected to combine a plan against this eventuality; and besides this, there were unhappy disputes between Kossuth, who advocated a line of conduct propounded by the party composed of the Polish military chiefs in the Hungarian service, and Geörgey and his officers, who were wholly devoted to him, and prepared to co-operate with all his views; so that there was no chief to combine and direct a clever movement by the whole force; and these reasons, amongst others, caused the Magyars to lose all the advantages now offered to them; and such opportunities as they had, never again presented themselves.

At the moment, therefore, when the Russian army was master of Kaschau and of the line of the Sajo, and the Austrians had concentrated themselves on the right bank of the Danube, and advanced in the direction of Comorn and Raab, it was found that the insurgent force was distributed, without plan or order, from the mouth of the Waag to Temesvar, being the full length of a line which cut the Danube and the Theiss diagonally. Geörgey with forty thousand men occupied the lower course of the Waag, on the left bank of the Danube; Klapka held Raab with twenty thousand men; Dembinsky with twenty thousand was posted between Szolnok and Alberti; Kmetz with fifteen thousand was in the environs of the Plattensee and Földwar; and thirty-five thousand men under Perczel and Guyon were concentrated at Szegedin and Thérésiopel; and eighteen thousand surrounded Arad and Temesvar. It was evident that this distribution of the Magyar forces would appear unfortunate as soon as the two allied armies should approach each other within an offensive march. The insurgent chiefs, however, hesitated in changing their position, and it was only at the last moment that they attempted a plan of concentration; but it was too late, and this military fault was decisive of the whole campaign; for it was the cause of the insurgent force being cut piecemeal by the onward movement of the Russian army. Pressed on in a diverging direction to the other side of the Theiss by the combined march of their adversaries towards Grosswardein and Temesvar, the two enervated trunks of the insurgent army were separately beaten, being either dispersed or forced to lay down their arms.

The operations of the allied armies seemed to present three principal points of view during this campaign. The first was their converging march from Kaschau and Raab, towards Waitzen and Pesth; a march which cut in pieces the line of operation of the insurgent army. The second was when Prince Paskiewitsch, in concentrating his army on the road of Hatvan to Miscolcz, and forcing the passage of the Theiss at Thissafured, became the pivot of the operations which had for object, on the north, to throw back the corps of Geörgey on Tokay, on the south, the army of Dembinski on Szegedin, and thus to cause the whole force to retire behind the Theiss. The third point of view was when the two principal armies, advancing concentrically by Grosswardein and Temesvar towards Arad, threw back the Magyars into the valley of the Marosch, where, attacked at the same time by the corps of General Lüders coming from Transylvania, it was forced, after various successes and defeats, to lay down its arms.

On the 26th of June, the young Austrian

Emperor repaired in person to the general quarters of the army, resolved to share its perils and victories.

The large body of insurgents under General Klapka had taken up their position under Raab, and occupied the trenches. The third corps of the Austrian army had been directed on Arpas to cross the Rabnitz, and come in contact, from the right hand, with the position of the Magyars at Raab; they took Czonok by assault, and continued their march by Telh and Tenyö.

General Haynau also began offensive operations against Raab; the first corps, and that of reserve, marched to the attack, and the Russian division under Paniutine, and a corps of cavalry, rested as reserve at Leyden and Sörvenyhaza. While General Schlik advanced from Hochstrass on the Abda to force the passage of the Rabnitz, General Wohlgemuth, with the reserve, advanced by Leswar along the left bank of this river. The insurgents who guarded the banks of the Abda, seeing themselves taken in flank, fired the bridge and retired; the young Emperor, who now arrived at this point of the field of battle, was the first to pass the river on the burning embers of the bridge; the troops followed the noble example of their Emperor with avidity; they advanced quickly to the trenches of Raab, and found but feeble resistance; the Magyars, finding that their line of retreat was menaced by the advance of the third corps, evacuated Raab, and retired towards Acs, under protection of the cannon on the *tête du pont* of Comorn.

After the occupation of Raab, the Austrian army and Russian division advanced towards Comorn and took up a position on the heights of Gönyö. Geörgey, after the retreat of his army from Raab, had been instructed by Kossuth to lead his troops to Pesth, for it was the intention of the insurgents to retire into Transylvania, and carry on the war there; but Geörgey returned for answer that the present positions of the enemy prevented him then from doing so; and that if he did at a later period, he could not then protect the capital against the enemy. This declaration was looked on with great suspicion by Kossuth and those with whom he took council, amongst whom were Perczel and Dembinski, and he resolved to remove Geörgey from the chief command and give it to Mészaros. Geörgey was consequently recalled, and the latter general installed in his post on the 1st of July. This fatal measure was most unfortunate for the Magyar cause, creating a deadly feud and division in the chiefs, when the strictest unity and friendship were indispensable to their successes. The troops idolized Geörgey, and looked to him alone for orders; and, although this general acquiesced in the commands of Kossuth, yet the troops never gave their confidence to his successor. Indeed, events marched so rapidly that there was no time for calm deliberation on plans or concerted action. Several councils of war were held, and Geörgey proposed to break through the enemy's line on the right bank of the Danube, and so pursue offensive operations; and advanced his views with so much show of reason, that he carried them against the decided opinion and advice of Klapka and others. This expedition again divided the Magyar forces, and weakened all their subsequent efforts.

Haynau was now informed that the insurgents, reinforced by considerable detachments, occupied a strong position between Acs and Comorn, under the personal command of Geörgey, and that they were in daily expectation of forty thousand men, marching from Buda. On the strength of this news, Haynau resolved on making a forced *reconnoissance*, with a view to hinder the junction of the two corps. He ordered the first corps of his own army, under Schlik, to march directly on Acs, and to attack the enemy in front; the reserve was to diverge to the right and manœuvre to the left of the insurgents—the third corps was to occupy Szem, and the road to Stuhlweissenberg; the division of cavalry was to extend itself on the high road, leading from Comorn to Pesth, and hinder the junction of the strong body of the enemy expected from that quarter, and the reserve of the artillery, and the Russian division should follow the movement of the Austrian reserve division. It was soon found, however, that the report of forty thousand men in support from Buda was exaggerated. At the approach of the Austrian corps from Comorn, Geörgey placed fifty pieces of artillery in battery, and supported them with twenty squadrons of hussars. The battle began, and the Austrians now found that they had a resolute enemy to deal with : on two points, however, they gained advantages ; but as they did not mean to accept a battle, but merely to ascertain the real strength of their opponents, they were but of little importance. At seven in the evening, Geörgey, excited by an audacious *coup de main* of a body of Austrian cavalry, and desirous of putting his plan into execution, operated an attack with twelve battalions, forty squadrons, and twelve batteries. He routed Schlik with great impetuosity, occupied the forest of Harkaly, and menaced the right flank of the Austrians. Schlik sent an express to the Russian division, which came up immediately in aid.

Covered by the small hills and undulating nature of the ground, the Russian detachment advanced on the left flank of the insurgents, to within range of their cannon, and having quickly placed their batteries, opened a murderous discharge against the Magyars ; the attack was so sudden and unexpected, and the immediate loss so great, that they were obliged to retreat in all haste. While this was being accomplished on the right bank of the river, the Magyars attacked the second corps of the Austrians on the left bank, but they had not the success desired. Geörgey, on the 2nd of July, became convinced that he could not shake the Austrian position on the right bank of the river; he changed his plan of operations and resolved to march quickly on Waitzen, by the left bank, and effect a junction of his army with Dembinski; to conceal his intention from his men, he operated a sortie from the *tête du pont* of the Danube, and this had a very beneficial effect; although opposed valiantly by the Austrians, their fourth corps was obliged to retreat on Szem, but the arrival of the Russian division Paniutine, at the most critical moment, turned the chances against the Magyars; they were advancing to a decisive attack, but the appearance of the compact and well-disciplined battalions of Russians on their left flank caused them to pause, and the effect of Russian artillery deciding them to retire, they withdrew to their intrenchments. During this combat Geörgey had already directed a part of his train by the left bank towards Grann, and he himself with the first, third, and seventh corps, marched on to Waitzen, hoping to join Perczel and Dembinski; Klapka, who commanded at Comorn, assisted this movement most effectively with a portion of his troops; but this brilliant idea of Geörgey was put in execution too late, a few days earlier it might have baffled the combinations of the allies; but, as it was, the allied armies,—the Austrians, being near Comorn, and the Russians at Gyöngyös, already communicated with each other, and on the 11th of July, a division of Austrians, supported by one of Russians, entered Pesth and Ofen. The Austrians were not aware of the departure of Geörgey for Waitzen until two days after he had left Comorn, so that it was too late to think of following him. Haynau, leaving to the Russian army the task of opposing Geörgey, broke up with his whole force (leaving one corps in observation of the fortress of Comorn) for Pesth, with the view of assisting the Ban, and succouring Temesvar.

Prince Paskiewitsch now learnt that Geörgey was at the head of forty-five thousand men and one hundred and twenty pieces of cannon, in the direction of Waitzen: there was no time to lose, three battalions and eight squadrons were ordered off by forced marches to observe the Magyars, but not to engage in a combat. The whole body of cavalry followed, as well as a large force of infantry, and precautions were taken against any attack by Perczel. Georgey, with his enormous forces, had driven every thing before him, until, at length, the two armies faced each other at Hartijan; and the insurgent general, seeing that he had to do with the whole of the Russian army, was not anxious for the combat.

Having left the first corps with General Nagy Sandor at Waitzen, to cover his movement, he gained the road to Balassa-Gyarmath in the night, with the remainder of his force. The Cossacks had surprised the advanced guard of the Magyars when their last column was retiring from Waitzen, and determined on entering the town; but they soon repented their hardihood, for they were assailed on all sides from the windows of the houses, the garrison of the place, and a large portion of Geörgey's army, which had returned for the purpose, and they were obliged to retire with celerity; but the column of General Rüdiger was already on its advance, and succeeded in annoying its enemy in its retiring movement. Prince Paskiewitsch followed Geörgey by a flying detachment under the orders of Generals Sass and Grabbe, and the principal army took the road from Pesth to Miskolcz in three columns, in the following order: the second corps, with the general quarters, removed to Azod, and detached its advanced guard towards Zsomber; Rüdiger, with the third corps, marched directly on Gyöngyös, and the fourth corps advanced from Kassolna on Nezö-Köwesd, with orders to push forward towards Harsany and Miskolcz. Thus the Prince gained the certain and decisive advantages of the combined support of the whole mass of Russian troops on the important line from Hatwan to Miskolcz. In occupying this position he expected to throw Geörgey towards Tokay, Perczel to Szolnok and on to the Austrian army in possession of Pesth, to serve as an efficient assistant to the movements of this latter towards Szegedin, and to remain for the moment quiescent, until a favourable opportunity should occur to enable him to strike a decisive blow in carrying his masses on to the important fortress of Grosswardein.

CHAPTER VI.

During the continuance of these energetic measures on the part of Austria, aided by Russia, for the subjugation of Hungary, the prosecution of the siege of Venice was not forgotten; but, from the extraordinary position of the city, it was a task of the greatest difficulty to make the least impression; and so long as there was a chance of the success of the Magyar cause, so long was Manin resolved to resist the attacks of the assailants.

But the successes of the Imperialists in Hungary now raised their most sanguine hopes of being enabled to put down the revolutionary element every where, and a corresponding increase of energy was infused into the minds of their military chiefs. It seemed almost a reproach to the Austrians that they had been so long before Venice and had yet accomplished so little; and it was only those who practically knew the immense difficulties to be overcome, who were able to appreciate the extraordinary exertions and perseverance of the Imperial army up to the present time. General William Pepe, who held the chief command within the city, had done all that an excellent officer could accomplish for its obstinate defence, and he was nobly seconded by those under his command, and the general body of the people, although frequently thwarted by the measures of government, of which Manin was still the head. The blockade continued most strictly throughout the winter; but it was not until the ensuing month of April that the Austrians were enabled to resume effective offensive measures.

In the beginning of May an uninterrupted fire from thirty cannon of large calibre opened on fort Malghera, and which lasted for upwards of twelve hours. New works were built, and others strengthened, and the city was now besieged in due form. The Imperialists prepared their greatest energies for the 26th of the month, and above one hundred pieces of artillery were ranged, and poured forth their fire against the devoted fort of Malghera; this cannonade produced great effect, for it was ascertained that the casemates at the fort were not proof against such an attack, and it was deemed necessary for the garrison to withdraw from the place. The Austrians were not aware that the fort was evacuated, and continued their fire during the whole of the night; but at length, finding that they were not answered, they entered early in the morning, and took possession. The Venetian garrison, on their return to the city, blew up many of the arches of the railway bridge, but not so effectually as they might have done; they raised an enormous barrier against the further advance of the Austrians, which was built of earth and sand banks, twenty-five feet high and fifty feet thick, and which they mounted with heavy guns, and raised works on either side for other cannon, so that the embankment had a most formidable appearance; they increased the fortifications of San Secundo, and put all their gun-boats into requisition. The Imperialists were not less active, and they also raised works, and attempted a bombardment of the city, but not with much success; for they were still at too great a distance from the interior for their shells to tell, although they now occupied the small isle of San Guiliano, in which they had raised a heavy battery. The works of the Austrians occupied a long period, and they changed their positions incessantly, in the hope that, at length, they might gain a point from which they might reach the interior of the city; they fired round shot at an elevation of nearly forty-five degrees, but were not even then successful in their object, for the distance was still above four thousand metres from the centre. The unfortunate inhabitants were reduced to the greatest extremities, living on the coarsest food and the smallest possible quantity. Manin and the other members of the government, had no intention of capitulating so long as they could really exist, for they always hoped for some change in their favour, and propagated many reports of the successes of the Hungarians, and discomfiture of the Austrians, to cheer the spirits of the famished population; neither newspapers nor letters had penetrated the lines for a length of time, so that the people were entirely at the mercy of their rulers, who invented and made public what it suited their interest to have believed.

By the 16th of July an immense train of heavy guns opened their fire against the batteries and the city itself, and the Imperialists endeavoured to gain possession of the enormous embankment by stratagem. About eighty soldiers stole along the side of the lagune and climbed up the bank of earth, without being discovered; when they appeared at the top, the Venetian guard, imagining that the whole force of the enemy was following, fled for their lives, and there was little doubt that, had this bold attempt been properly seconded at once, it would have been crowned with success; but the party made but a small show when assembled at the top of the barrier, which being perceived by the Venetians, they returned in great numbers, and compelled their assailants to a speedy retreat. About the 26th the Imperialists resolved to make one more energetic attempt against the city; and Radetzky himself having now arrived at the scene of action, the military vied with each other in valour and enthusiasm. On the 29th a perfect storm of shell and shot commenced, and continued, with scarcely any intermission, until the 24th of August. The sufferings of the wretched inhabitants were extreme, and although the city could yet have held out, they were not proof against the accumulated miseries of starvation, fever, and cholera; it was computed that from this latter scourge alone two hundred died every day, and provisions were now utterly exhausted; in this horrid dilemma, the government sent a deputation to General

Gorskouski, who had the immediate charge of the siege, and terms of capitulation were discussed; nothing, however, having been definitively settled, the bombardment was continued until the 22nd, and on this day the deputation again proceeded to the Austrian head quarters, and at length conditions were proposed on the one hand and accepted on the other, to the effect that, an unconditional surrender of the city should be given; that all forts, arms, and ammunition be delivered up; that all persons compromised by the revolution have permission to leave by sea or land; and that a pardon be granted to all soldiers and officers who had defended the city; and on the morning of the 23rd the Austrians took possession, not a little gratified to obtain it on any terms.

We must now turn our attention again to Hungary, where the last throes of the revolutionary movement in the Austrian empire were now vibrating. The Russian army, under Prince Paskiewitsch, had assumed so advantageous a position, in consequence of his late successful battle, that the Magyars felt themselves most critically exposed; and the results of the combinations detailed at the end of the last chapter, verified the assertion of the Russian commander, that the revolution would now be soon successfully put down. In conformity with the dispositions ordered, the Russian quarter-general and the second corps of infantry arrived at Aszod, where the advanced guard met with the Magyar outposts. Perczel and Wysocki, who debouched from Szolnok with twenty thousand men, had marched with their advanced guard, consisting of thirty-two squadrons, and fourteen pieces of cannon, in this direction. The Russians were energetically attacked, and were on the point of retiring, when a division of infantry, arriving at the critical moment to their assistance, and advancing quickly to the charge under protection of the artillery, caused the Magyars to retreat, who, in this unfortunate *melée*, lost a considerable number of men and baggage. Disconcerted by the issue of this attack, The Hungarian commander-in-chief retired towards Szegedin, and the Russian commander seized the advantages now offered him, and marched with the second and third corps by Gyöngyös, on Kapolna; thus being enabled on the one side to effectuate the passage of the Theiss, and open the road to Debreczin for their further advance, and on the other, to support the different corps sent to operate against Geörgey.

These corps were disposed thus: the detachment of Sass and Grabbe followed Geörgey; the fourth corps, under Tchéodajeff, had attained Mezo Kowesdé, and marched on Miskolcz, and General Saaken descended by forced marches by Eperies on Kaschau and Hydas-Nemethy; the marching orders of these corps were calculated so that they should attain the Sajo at the same time as Geörgey; and there, by combining their movements, should present an imposing mass, which, if not able to strike a decisive blow, should yet hinder that general from establishing himself on the line of communication of the great Magyar army, and envelop him in the network of the Russian operations. Prince Paskiewitsch sent a division under General Gortschakoff to force the passage of the Theiss, and which soon appeared before Poroszlo. Here a Magyar force of five thousand men, two squadron of hussars, and ten pieces of artillery, was posted under the orders of Kortunay; but after a severe battle, the Russians were successful in re-establishing the bridges which had been destroyed by their enemy, and crossed the river. Thus master of the road to Debreczin, the Russian commander-in-chief waited only the result of the operations directed against Geörgey; but Grabbe, not having received his definitive orders, took upon him to direct his division on Neusohl, with the view of checking Geörgey on the road to the plain of Schemnitz. Having, however, later received his instructions, he found he could only attain the neighbourhood of Geörgey after this latter general had succeeded in passing Rima-Szombat, and debouched into the valley of the Sajo. Followed closely in his retrograde movement by Sass, Geörgey could not retire without experiencing considerable loss in train and munitions, but he arrived at Putnok, and here reformed his troops, and, dividing them into two columns, directed one towards Forro, and with the other he marched on Miskolcz. Théojadeff, who had attained this locality, moved on to meet him. Geörgey, after a skirmish with him, passed on to the left bank of the Sajo, and broke the bridges, and the Russian general thought it prudent to take the road to Ahrany to draw near to the principal part of his army. By this time Grabbe had debouched on Miskolcz and crossed the Sajo, and a lively affair took place between him and Geörgey ; but the Russian general, finding that he had to do with a strong force of the enemy, retired to wait for a junction with Saaken, to enable him again to take the offensive. Prince Paskiewitsch now caused a second bridge to be erected at Csege, and transported the second corps of his army. This movement, and the near approach of General Saaken, took Geörgey by surprise, and he hastened to cross the Theiss, and directed himself towards Debreczin. Saaken occupied Tokay, and re-established the broken bridge over the Theiss, and the fourth corps was advanced on the road from Kaschau to Debreczin, to ensure the desired communication of the army in general. The Prince, at the head of the second and third corps, crossed the bridge at Csege, attained Ujvaros on the 1st of August, and directed himself, the next day, on Debreczin. This city was now occupied by a column of Geörgey's army amounting to eighteen thousand men, and forty pieces of cannon commanded by Nagy Sandor; and he, resolving to resist to the last, opened a lively cannonade against the Russian force, and a furious battle ensued; but overpowered by numbers and especially by the murderous fire of the Russian artillery, the Magyars were beaten, and obliged to retire. By the 3rd of August Prince Paskiewitsch had concentrated the second and third corps and the twelfth division of infantry at Debreczin, and there waited for news of the operations of General Haynau. The Austrian army had on this day crossed the Theiss, and occupied Szegedin, and had disposed itself to march to the succour of Temeswar. Geörgey also took a direction towards this fortress and that of Arad, and Prince Paskiewitsch ordered the third corps to take possession of Grosswardein; and General Rudiger, with this corps, occupied the city on the 8th of August. A strong body of cavalry was now detached against Geörgey, and a second advanced guard directed to Gross-Salantha, on the road to Arad, to open communication with the Austrian army.

A few moments must, however, now be devoted to the military events passing in Transylvania, and also to the movements of the principal part of the Austrian army under General Haynau. Two Russian corps had received orders to penetrate,—the one from Wallachia, the other from Bucowina—into Transylvania, to subdue this province, and then to combine their ulterior movements with the principal army. One corps was opposed by the Magyar chief Kiss, who guarded the defile of Tomosch. The Russians advanced to this spot; but here they were warmly met, and it was not without great loss that they succeeded in occupying this position; but after a heroic resistance, Kiss was routed, and himself taken prisoner. The occupation of Cronstadt was the immediate result of this victory. The second Russian corps marched by Ruko on Rosenau, and, after dispersing three thousand Magyars, occupied this town. The Russians, after the occupation of Cronstadt, proceeded to disarm the country of the Szeklers; and their commander sent word to the Austrian General Clamm to advance and occupy this city with his troops, while they should be thus employed; and then the Russians resolved to march on Hermannstadt. The Magyars held the passage of the Rothenthurm with two thousand men and eight pieces of cannon, but were obliged to retire on to Turkish ground, where they laid down their arms, which were delivered to General Lüders. Hermannstadt surrendered to the Russian force; but General Bem, having concentrated about twenty thousand men and fourteen pieces of cannon, resolved to renew the tactics which had been so successful before against the Austrians, by marching direct to the North, and throwing back the Russian detachment into Bucowina, to descend at once to the south, and there direct all his efforts against the enemy—but he had not now the same success. However, finding that Cronstadt was only occupied by an Austrian detachment, he resolved to try his fortune against that place; but General Clamm resolutely went out to meet him, and attacking him vigorously, compelled him to renounce all projects against that fortress. Seeing so active an enemy as Bem in the field, General Lüders resolved to attempt to impede any plan of this able general, by a movement on Maros-Vasarhely; and, joining the division of General Clamm with his own, took his dispositions accordingly. Here Bem appeared, with about ten thousand men and twelve pieces of cannon. After a murderous battle, in the early part of which the Russian General Scariatine lost his life, the Russian artillery again decided the combat in their favour; and Bem was obliged to retreat, with the loss of one thousand men dead, five hundred prisoners, eleven cannon, and four cases of munition; two standards and a large quantity of arms and baggage, together with the carriage of Bem himself, fell into the hands of the Russians. This battle was called the victory of Segesvar, and was a decisive stroke against the further successful resistance of General Bem. But this officer was not to be beaten so easily; he reached Maros-Vasarhely, and here assembled all his disposable force; he obtained a re-inforcement of four thousand men and twelve pieces of cannon, and put himself in motion towards Galfalwa; but changing his course, he suddenly appeared before Hermannstadt, and entered it on the 6th of August. The Russians followed closely, having the same intention; but, seeing the place occupied by their enemy, they ranged themselves in order of battle in the neighbourhood. Bem resolutely went out of the city to meet them, with a portion of his troops; but he was not successful, and being repulsed on all sides, he retired as far as Grossau. This defeat of Bem at Hermannstadt struck down the insurrection in Transylvania; and the continued successes of the Russian corps prognosticated the early submission of the whole province. General Lüders, therefore, resolved on leaving the country in the hands of General Clamm, and proceeded to combine his movements with the principal armies in Hungary; and, after more successes, he appeared on the ground of the theatre of war at the decisive moment, and completed the operations of the two armies, having crowned the Austro-Russian campaign by relieving Transylvania entirely from Magyar influence.

A few words, on the operations of the Austrian army accompanied by the Russian division under General Pianutine, will complete this *coup d'œil* of the movements of the whole armies. The Austrians, as we have stated, under General Haynau, were on their road to Temesvar, and the Magyar troops under Dembinski had retrograded towards Szegedin. The first operations of the Austrians were favourable, and had an important result; for Dembinski, having seen the necessity of concentrating the whole of his disposable force for the defence of the passage of the Theiss, the corps under General Guyon, which had hitherto kept the Ban Jellacic in check, was ordered, equally with all others at the disposition of Dembinski, to quit its position, and remove to Szegedin. Guyon could have rendered abortive all attempts of the Ban to advance, but for the approach of the Austrian army under Haynau. The march of this latter general on Szegedin, therefore, opened a communication between Jellacic and himself; and the latter, having now his right wing protected, was enabled to pursue his operations with less anxiety. Dembinski had the intention of defending Szegedin to the last extremity; but, on the near approach of the combined army, they found that part of the town, situated on the right bank of the Theiss, unoccupied by the Magyars — who seemed resolved to dispute the passage of the river. Haynau made his dispositions for an energetic attack, and attempted the passage with boldness; and, after some hard fighting, he succeeded in establishing a bridge. But, towards the evening, the

Magyars returned to the charge, and made a most violent attack on the *tête du pont.* Here the Russian division was put forward in support of the Austrians, and by ten at night the Magyar columns retired. The allied army now advanced over the bridge against the enemy, drawn up in a strong position near Szoreg and St. Iwan, to the number of thirty thousand men and fifty pieces of cannon, and commanded by Dembinski, Meszaros, Desewffy, and Guyon. The Magyars, after some fighting, again changed their position in part; but the first corps of the Austrian army, which had fortunately crossed the Theiss at another point, now attained Mako, and threatened the communications of the Magyar army. Checked in front by the principal column of the Austrians under Haynau, and menaced on either side laterally by the movements of the two columns of the first and third corps, the Magyars made a precipitate retreat on Temesvar.

Although numerically strong, it was evident to the allies that the Magyars were in great disorder and discouragement; but they, having still one hundred cannon at command, resolved to try the fortune of a battle under the walls of Temesvar. Bem had arrived from Transylvania, and given his valuable assistance in the movements of the Magyar army, consequent on this determination, but fortune no longer smiled upon them; and, although a most desperate battle took place between the two armies, and prodigies of valour were performed, and evolutions executed which would have done honour to the talents of the ablest generals, the allied army gained a most decided victory. The artillery played the most conspicuous part on both sides; but this arm of the service, in the hands of the Russians, was employed in the most scientific manner in crushing masses, and decided the victory in their favour. General Haynau penetrated into Temesvar, and thus relieved this fortress from the great straits it had so long endured. He dispatched General Schlik to gain possession of Arad, and join communication with the principal Russian army, and made his dispositions for the pursuit of the Magyar force, which retired rapidly on Lugos.

As we have seen, at this same period Prince Paskiewitsch, after the victory of Debreczin on the 2nd of August, occupied Grosswardein with the principal Russian army, and had thrown forward a strong column, under the orders of General Rüdiger, to watch the movements of Geörgey. General Lüders, also, after having routed the army under Bem, in Transylvania, debouched by Dewa into the valley of the Maros, while another Russian column occupied Clausenberg, ready to assist their brethren at Grosswardein. By these combined movements, the allied masses pressed the insurrection into an iron circle, which contracted from day to day. The different Magyar columns, beaten and harassed by successive defeats and constant changes of position, were undecided and restless. The columns of Geörgey were sheltered under the cannon of Arad. Those of Dembinski and Bem had gained Lugos and the grand route of Karanseles and Turkey; but the numerous train, and quantities of material left on their march, betrayed their disorganization and weakness.

But, while the unavoidable catastrophe was thus advancing at this point, the hopes of the Magyar party received a momentary gleam of sunshine from a most unexpected success of that part of the army still in garrison at Comorn. General Czorich was in observation of this fortress, with the second corps of the Austrian army. The garrison consisted of thirty thousand men, commanded by General

Klapka; and they possessed the *têtes du pont* of the Danube and Waag. This general now resolved to use his advantages, and endeavour to redeem the misfortunes of his brethren in arms elsewhere. On the 30th of July he debouched in great strength on the left side, between the Waag and the Danube, and threw his enemy back, behind the former river. Advancing with eight thousand men, eight squadrons, and twenty-four pieces, he carried every thing before him, and the Austrians retired in confusion: the right bank of the Danube remained completely at his mercy, and he entered and took possession of the city of Raab. By this success he gained thirty pieces of cannon, and great *depôts* of provisions and munitions of war. Czorich retired precipitately on Presburg, and caused an extraordinary alarm to the government at Vienna. A complete panic struck the inhabitants, who now thought that the insurrectionary cause was triumphant; and the most painful impressions were created everywhere. Hasty but numerous reinforcements were pushed on from all parts towards Presburg, and General Gyulay, the Minister of War, personally took the command; and by dint of the greatest energy and perseverance showed such a front that General Klapka did not care to push his victorious march too far from the fortress of Comorn.

Had these measures been adopted and carried into execution at an earlier period by this general, it is not improbable that they would have had an extraordinary effect on the war in general; but, as it was, the successes of the allied armies were of too decided a nature for such a fortuitous circumstance as we have now described to restrain the final catastrophe. Obliged to flee from Pesth and Szegedin, and from this latter city to Arad, the revolutionary government became errant, and lost all its influence. The want of time to establish the presses for the continuation of coining paper money deprived the government of pecuniary resources, and augmented the discredit into which it had fallen.

At Arad Kossuth had flattered himself that by making this fortress the centre of the further operations of the army, and of the action of the revolutionary government, he could re-establish the fluctuating chances of the rebellion in his favour—but this illusion speedily disappeared. Tired of war, the people were ready to submit at any price; a large portion of Kossuth's partizans had the same feeling, the army itself was in rapid decay, and would neither obey the decrees of the government, or further defend itself. While Dembinski had retired in disorder on Temesvar, there to be defeated as we have seen, Nagy Sandor, forming the advanced guard of Geörgey's army, had, on the 8th of August, arrived near Arad; but the corps he commanded, demoralised and completely chilled by its recent defeat at Debreczin, would not stand before the column of General Schlik opposed to it, and retired hastily on the right bank of the Maros. Georgey on the next day, approached Arad with his troops; but having received the intelligence of the defeat of Dembinski and Bem at Temesvar, and their retreat to Lugos, and the consequent advance of the Russian force, under General Rüdiger, he found that he was placed in a most critical position.

Kossuth saw that all chance of success had vanished! Dembinski in flight towards Lugos—Georgey in full retreat on Villagos —what was to be done? The dictator, with the consent of the council called for the purpose of deliberating on the serious aspect of affairs, sent General Poltenberg, to Prince Paskiewitsch to treat for peace; the non-success of this mission having proved to the provisional government that an unconditional surrender could only avail, Kossuth resolved to resign his powers into Geörgey's hands; and on this event taking place, he issued a manifesto, which was signed by the other members of the government, and addressed to the Hungarian nation, in the following words: "After the unfortunate battles by which, lately, God has scourged the people of Hungary, I have no hope of continuing the defence of the country with any chance of success against the enormous forces of Austria and Russia combined. In this state of things, the situation of the country, and the well-being of its futurity, depend solely on the exertions of the general commanding the army, and I am of opinion that the prolonged existence of the government would not only be useless, but prejudicial to the country at large. I therefore, by this manifesto, make known to the nation, as well personally as in the name of the entire government, that, animated by those patriotic sentiments which have ever guided me, and which have produced the immense sacrifices I have ever made for the public good, I hereby retire from the government; and further, that I invest General Arthur Geörgey with the supreme power, both civil and military, for so long a period as the nation, using its undoubted rights, should not otherwise resolve. I expect that General Arthur Geörgey (and I render him responsible before God and his country for his conduct) will employ this supreme power now invested in him according to the best of his ability, to ensure the national independence of the country. May he, as well as myself, yet have the happiness of laying the foundations for the future prosperity of the country. I can no longer be useful to my country by my active exertions—if my death should be deemed an advantage, I am willing to sacrifice my life to attain it. May the God of justice and mercy yet protect the country!"

Geörgey being thus invested with the supreme command, issued the following proclamation:

"The provisional government has ceased to exist—the dictator and his ministers have voluntarily renounced their post. In this state of things, a military distatorship is indispensable; I therefore accept this position as well as that of the civil power.—Citizens! all that can be done in the unfortunate situation of the country, will I, either by a continuation of the war, or by pacific means, effect. Citizens! the late events are extraordinary and unexpected, and the strokes of destiny fearful. It is impossible, at present, to see into the future. My sole desire is that you should all quietly retire to your homes, and think no more of resistance; even when the enemy shall be in possession of your cities, you will have the greater chance of safety for yourselves and property, by remaining near your homesteads and flocks, and in occupying yourselves with your usual domestic duties. Citizens! what God, in his inscrutable designs, has laid on the country, we must bear with sturdy resolution, and with the firm conviction that right cannot be hidden for all eternity!"

Knowing, therefore, the impossibility of a longer resistance, Geörgey, on the 12th of August, made known the resolution he had come to for an unconditional submission to General Rüdiger. This important act took place the next day, at Villagos, and thirty thousand men, with one hundred and forty-four pieces of cannon, and eight thousand horse, submitted to the Russian power. The commanders of the fortresses of Arad and Peterwardein followed the example of their chief; but Comorn still held out.

Dembinski having divided his army at Lugos, one part took the direction to Deva, the other the road to Karansebes.

Followed by a brigade under General Simbschen, a portion of the latter force, amounting to five thousand men and nineteen pieces, laid down their arms at Karansebes. The first column abandoned to Prince Liechtenstein seventy-two pieces of cannon and one hundred ammunition waggons; and another part of this corps, of about seven thousand five hundred men with five hundred and five officers, two cannon, eight standards and one thousand and sixty-seven horses rendered at discretion to General Rüdiger at Kis-Jenö; two thousand more of the men gave themselves up as prisoners at Grosswardein. Bem and Guyon, bolder and more sanguine than the rest, had retired by the valley of the Maros as far as Dobra, in the hope of again tempting the God of battles in their favour against the troops of General Lüders, but their men refused to fight any longer. These generals were constrained therefore to flee, and twelve battalions of infantry, eight squadrons of cavalry and fifty-two pieces of cannon here surrendered. Comorn was now the only place standing out; but after a time a capitulation was agreed on, the garrison with their officers received a free marching off, and the Austrians took possession of this last stronghold of the revolutionary party.

In this way was the insurrection of the Magyars put down. But alas! for the kingdom of Hungary! many years of peace and prosperity will not restore her to what she was; and should Austria even succeed in incorporating her into its "united kingdom," under the constitution of the 4th March, 1849, she will ever remain a festering thorn in her side; for the proud spirit of the Magyar must always continue in bitter opposition to Austrian rule!

In the subsequent courts martial on those prisoners in the hands of the Austrians, and those delivered up to them by the

Russians, figure the time-honoured names of Louis Batthyanyi (shot), Louis Aulich (hung), Ernest Kiss (shot), John Damjanistch (hung), Ignaz Torok (hung), Joseph Nagy Sandor (hung), Charles Vecsey (hung), Charles Knesich (hung), George Lahner (hung), Ernest von Poltenberg (hung), Charles Leinengen-Westerberg (hung), William Lazar (hung), Aristedes Desewffy (hung), Joseph Schweidel (hung), and the high-minded Ladislas Czanyi. All these, and many others, suffered death at the hands of their ruthless conquerors, while Louis Kossuth, Meszaros, Dembinski, Bem, Casimir Batthyanyi, Guyon, and other officers, with five thousand men, fled to the frontier, and delivered themselves into the hands of the Turks, who, after a long negociation with Austria, transferred them to Schumla as prisoners, and placed them under the care of a strong military guard, where they (with the exception of Bem and a few others who embraced Mohammedanism, and thus obtained their personal liberty) will, in all probability, waste the remainder of their eventful lives in hopeless captivity.

THE END.

J. BILLING, PRINTER, WOKING.

IV.

WARKWORTH CASTLE;

A HISTORICAL ROMANCE.

"The book is what might have been expected from a disciple of Mr. G. P. R. James—it is not unlikely to find a numerous circle of admirers."—*Daily News Express.*

"Proves that the author has drunk deeply at the sources whereat Porter, Scott, and G. P. R. James drew their inspiration."—*Weekly Chronicle.*

"Scott once removed."—*Spectator.*

V.

MASTERS AND WORKMEN;

A TALE,

Illustrative of the Social and Rural Condition of the People.

By LORD B——

"A very clever novel."—*Spectator.*

"A novel of the highest order—a novel that ought to be read by all grades of society. The moral and social lessons it enforces, if acted upon, would render the English people more happy and contented—would give the master and workman, the rich and the poor, a greater interest in each other's welfare."—*New York Herald.*

"The work has great interest."—*Daily News Express.*

VI.

TALVI'S HISTORY OF

THE COLONIZATION OF AMERICA.

By WILLIAM HAZLITT, Esq., of the Inner Temple.

VII.

KAMENSKI'S AGE OF PETER THE GREAT.

By IVAN GOLOVINE,

Author of "The Russian Sketch Book," &c.

VIII.

In Two Vols. 21s.

THE PASTORS IN THE WILDERNESS.

A HISTORY of the HUGUENOTS, from the REVOCATION of the EDICT of NANTES to the FIRST FRENCH REVOLUTION. By a LUTHERAN DIVINE.

IX.

In Three Vols.

FERNLEY MANOR;

A NOVEL. By Mrs. MACKENZIE DANIELS, Author of "My Sister Minnie," "Our Guardian," &c.

X.

In Two Vols. 21s.

SUPERNATURAL ILLUSIONS.

Printed uniform with "The Night Side of Nature," by Mrs. CROWE, to which it will form a Sequel.

XI.

A Second Edition. Price 5s.

THE ROCK OF ROME.

By J. SHERIDAN KNOWLES, Author of "The Hunchback," "The Wife," &c.

XII.

A Second Edition. In One Vol. with plates, 7s. 6d.

EXMOOR.

By MAJOR BYNG HALL.

XIII.

In the Press. In Three Vols.

CATHERINE ERLOP.

A NOVEL. By Mrs. STEWARD, Author of "The Prediction," &c. &c.

759743

Printed in Great Britain by
Amazon.co.uk, Ltd.,
Marston Gate.